Be The First Believer

A Collection Of Leadership Lessons For Life

Ed Deutschlander and Rich Campe

Be The First Believer

www.Northstarfinancial.com
www.Proadvisorcoach.com

Isbn: 978-0-578-12604-3

Printed by Bethany Press International

Printed in the United States of America.

PRAISE FROM TOP PROFESSIONALS AND LEADERS FOR

Be The First Believer

"I have been around great people all my life, in sports, business and industry. I have seen men and women with the "It" factor for a long time. Simply put, Rich & Ed have the "It" factor and that will become obvious as you enjoy the powerful expression of their greatness in Be The First Believer. Something about them sets them apart from the crowd, and there is much more power when you get two people together that have the "It" factor like Rich and Ed have done with this book.

I hope you find this book insightful, powerful and life-changing as you become your first believer."

- Walter Bond, Former NBA Athlete,
World's Preeminent Expert on Sales,
Motivation and Leadership,
"Mr. Accountability", TV Host
"Giving You the Business", the Food Network

"Ed is one of the great field leaders in the financial services industry. Rich is an incredible coach and thought leader. Together, they are an unstoppable team. Ed's mind is like an avalanche of ideas and Rich has helped him capture his best in this easy to read

format. Whether you are just getting started in your career, or, you are the CEO of a major company, this book can act as a hand guide on leadership - nothing is left out!

- David W. Karr, CFPâ, ChFC, CLU
Co-President & Managing Partner, Karr Barth Associates Inc.

"Rich Campe and Ed Deutschlander's book Be the First Believer is a must read for anyone that wants a clear path to becoming a great leader while building a successful practice. The format makes for an easy read but most importantly the ideas can be implemented immediately to help grow your business. This book will have a permanent place in my library!"

- William D. "Bo" Keltner, CLU, CLF, FIC, LUTCF
Director & Regional Director,
Modern Woodmen Fraternal Financial

"Both Rich and Ed are leaders in their respective industries. My belief is they achieved and maintain that status because of what they believe to be true of themselves and those they lead. This book will provide you the clarity, certainty and confidence to believe you can accomplish what you set your heart and mind to achieving. Think of this as your blueprint for success and make sure it's not just in your library but on your desk at the ready. It's packed with sage advice from two amazing men. Read this book and enjoy what's really possible for you in this life when you BELIEVE!"

- Machen MacDonald, #1 Bestselling Author,
Coach and Speaker, ProBrilliance Leadership Institute

"Having read numerous books on personal development and leadership, Ed Deutschlander and Rich Campe have captured the very essence of what it takes in today's world to accomplish all that one wants to. Their plain-language, high energy book Be The First Believer is a detailed step- by- step plan that everyone can use to become a true visionary leader in the 21st century. No matter where one is in their career, the ways and means outlined can and will help individuals in all walks of life form the right habits, mindset and perspective as they go through their various endeavors in life."

- Bob Baccigalupi, past president GAMA International

"Be the First Believer is a testament to Ed Deutschlandar, one of our industry's foremost thought leaders. Ed and Rich have shared with us stories and lessons that help remind us of important principles that will surely impact the reader's walk as a leader."

- Daralee Barbera, CFP, CMFC, CLF, Managing Principal, Waddell & Reed, Inc.

"Be The First Believer is an invaluable tool for those who lead, while also inspiring the next generation of leaders."

- Tom Burns, CLU, ChFC, Chief Distribution Officer, Allianz Life Insurance Company of North America

"As a "Believer" myself, I enthusiastically encourage all people with unfulfilled dreams, and the ambition to achieve them, to read this wonderful book. The delightful anecdotes, illustrating the necessary traits for success, are a checklist for how to effectively attain one's life aspirations. I wish I had had the wisdom in this publication, instead of having wasted lots of time and money through trial and error procedures, to learn what is printed here in."

- Norman G. Levine CLU, ChFC, RFC. & President of Levine Enterprises

"A tremendous compilation of successful concepts, guiding precepts, and important ideas that will benefit anyone of any age. This is truly a "roadmap" for success not only in business, but in life. I'm getting copies for my family members and business associates in hopes they will read and learn from this important book."

- William E. Griffith, CLU, ChFC, Regional Managing Director, Principal Financial Group

"For those who desire to be a better mentor or could benefit from being mentored, there is no better place than this book to capitalize on the proven philosophies of a true "Mentored Mentor." We are fortunate that Ed Deutschlander has lead, and will continue to lead, this industry. His insight into seemingly simple situations insures we will not erode our fundamentals and continue to impact those we encounter in a positive manner."

- Mark A. Bonnett, Partner, Senior Vice President*, North Star Resource Group

"Rich Campe and I first met over 10 years ago and we had an immediate connection... as we like to say... "We are Brother's from another Mother". I have the deepest respect for Rich as a Friend, Family Man, Business Partner and Industry Leader. Rich does everything with Passion, Purpose and the Pursuit of Excellence! This book is a testimony to his relentless pursuit of giving back to others while leaving a legacy for generations to come. I would highly recommend you digest every page over and over to let the time tested principals synch in"."

- Leonard T. Wheeler, Formal NFL Veteran
NFL PA Board Member,
NFL PA Association Finance Committee
NFL Ambassador, Global Business Executive
Coach and Speaker

"Whether you are a young upcoming leader or an experienced executive, this book will help you "sharpen your saw"!! Ed Deutschlander's remarks reminded me of why I do what I do. It will help you create the "unique advantage" as you continue to development into the great leader that is inside all of us."

- Diane Yohn, Executive Vice President,
North Star Resource Group

"Rich has helped transform our firm by teaching us to let go of our limiting beliefs and have the confidence to achieve a bigger future! He is the "Ultimate Coach" for building a winning team, particularly if you want to see exponential growth. This book is an arsenal of best practices on how to get the most out of your organization and yourself. It is a must read!"

- Timothy J. Maguire, CFP, CLU
Co-President and Managing Partner,
Karr Barth Associates

"Finding good leadership role models in any walk of life are real problems we have in today's world. Be the First Believer brings together the people, values, habits and perspectives needed to help fill that void in our society. Any book of Ed Deutschlander's is a book you need to read."

- Conk Buckley CLU; CHFC, Hall of Fame;
Past Gama President, Essentials of Management facilitator

"After a struggle, Rich Campe was able to convince me that I could benefit from incorporating a coach into my practice. Since then, I have been absolutely amazed at what I have learned, what I have accomplished, and where I now believe, I can go. Without Rich's guidance and insight in almost every aspect of my business, I would not even realize how bright the future is. The sky has become the limit and I have Rich Campe to thank for it!"

- Andrew R. Avellan, CFP®, Director,
Certified Financial Planner™ Professional

"Be The First Believer is a great, relevant collection of the key things in life that you need to do to be successful in business and life. Ed shares simple stories, quotes and wisdom to really help a person, in any profession, understand the keys to making it in the real world."

- Marshall W. Gifford, CLU, ChFC, Senior Partner
Founder - North Star Medical Division,
North Star Resource Group

"If I have learned anything from building my 22 million dollar business and being an entrepreneur all my life, it's that we must constantly improve and never get complacent. Rich Campe exemplifies this Leadership quality in his heart and soul by never settling for just great. He strives every day to listen, learn and is always sharpening his blade to leave an everlasting legacy of extraordinary."

- Mike Agugliaro, CEO Gold Medal Service

"Most of the individuals who write or give seminars about leadership, have never led anything of significance. Their knowledge is purely theoretical or academic. They have no real world accomplishments that demonstrate their self-proclaimed skills. Ed Deutschlander is one of the very few teacher/coaches who has proven his superior, transferable leadership skills again and again in every dimension of his life. There is no one better than Ed to learn the "Principles of Leadership" from."

- Howard Elias, Chairman/CEO,
Wealth Advisory Group LLC

"I have known Rich for over a decade and I can say without a doubt that he gives 110% to everything he does. His coaching expertise has had a positive and profound impact on my life both professionally and personally. Rich has a way of drawing out the best from everyone he comes in contact with and clearly this book, Be The First Believer, does just that. Be The First Believer is a masterpiece and should be a cornerstone for anyone committed to great leadership."

- Brian Chapman, Capital Guardian, LLC, President, Independent Channel

"Ed Deutschlander inspires me with his wisdom and insight each time we are together. In Be the First Believer, he has created a simple and powerful framework that, if embraced, will dramatically elevate your career - and more importantly, your life."

- Kathryn L. Kellam, Chief Executive Officer, GAMA Foundation for Education + Research

"Be the First Believer is the type of book that busy people love! It is filled with amazing content that you can put to use immediately. If you have ever wanted the opportunity to sit and talk in detail about business strategies with two of the sharpest minds I have ever met, Rich Campe has written it down for you to keep in this book. It is a must read!

- Jonathan Marsh FIC, CFFM. CLF, Managing Partner Modern Woodmen Fraternal Financial, Top Manager 2010, 2011, 2012

"Ed Deutschlander's tremendous enthusiasm and energy are contagious and make him one of the great leaders in the financial services industry. His mind is like an avalanche of ideas and this book captures his best! Whether you are a CEO or just getting started in your career, it can serve as a handbook on how to be a great person and leader - nothing is left out."

- David W. Karr, CFPâ, ChFC, CLU, Co-President & Managing Partner, Karr Barth Associates Inc.

"Be The First Believer is an inspirational compilation of short interesting stories and anecdotes with a powerful message of tried and true leadership and life principles. This is not the typical leadership text book, but quick and profound lessons that can be easily remembered and applied for anyone of any age. I especially liked the stories about moving the big rocks first and why it's ok to be a little bit out of control. This will become the "Go To" book for professionals and parents to provide a blueprint for the future of their organizations and families.

Co-Author, Rich Campe is the perfect person to write this book. He doesn't just talk about these principles; he lives it by playing full out in every aspect of life. His energy, excitement and enthusiasm are contagious and impact everyone he meets. I never met anyone so committed to helping people discover their God given talents and strengths so they can strive to achieve their human greatness. I am proud to call Rich my coach, colleague and friend.

- Jamie Croland, Attorney, Certified Financial Planner™
Certified Business Coach

"Deutchlander's advice is brilliant. His book gives you a collection of small, simple tools that anyone can incorporate into their daily lives to achieve big results. I am adding it to the required reading list in my mentoring program."

- Howard Cowan, President, Cowan Financial Group

"Throughout my career from working for my dad at the family restaurant in the late 80's as a teenager, to be the #1 AXA Advisor in 2012, I have learned that great leaders are committed to always improving, a relentless pursuit of becoming better and never getting complacent. This book, Be The First Believer, is mandatory for all leaders who are just getting started or top of their field. Rich Campe, my coach, walks the talk and leads by example in this thought provoking masterpiece of easy to digest leadership seeds of greatness. A must read!"

- Thomas Mingone, ChFC,CLU,AEP,CFS
Managing Partner Capital Management Group of NY

"Ed's Leadership in the financial services industry and in his community has been an Inspiration and role model for me. You too will be inspired to be a better leader reading this book!"

- John Natoli, CFP®, CLU, ChFC, CMFC, CLF,
General Manager, Capstone Partners
Financial and Insurance Services, LLC,
MassMutual - Southern California Agency

"Be the First Believer is an outstanding compilation of some of the best, field tested leadership strategies in the industry. Presented in an easy to read format these strategies are simple yet powerfully effective. Whether you are looking to improve your own leadership skills or want to help develop these skills in others this book is a must read and a ready reference for anyone serious about leadership."

- David Vasos, Registered Principal*, President,
Chief Financial Officer, Chief Operating Officer,
North Star Resource Group

"One of the greatest gifts a person can have is the ability to help people see the best version of them self. Ed Deutschlander has spent his life influencing people in a profoundly positive way by coaching and believing in them before they believed in themselves. Be The First Believer is a continuation of that legacy and a gift to the world. Read it, live it, and give it someone you care about."

-Greg Smith, Senior Statewide Sales Director,
Farm Bureau Insurance of Michigan

"Be the First Believer exemplifies Ed Deutschlander's passion and enthusiasm in the field of leadership. As you read this book you can feel the incredible energy and emotion that makes Ed a true leader! This is a must read for anyone who wishes to experience success in life!"

-Athan Vorilas, CLU, CMFC, CLTC,
President/Managing Partner,
Lighthouse Financial Network, LLC

"Ed's book of lessons is indicative of his generosity and inspiration. He has personally impacted my life and now people he will

never meet, will be impacted by this great collection. Be The First Believer is a must read for anyone seeking excellence anywhere in their life, very well done!"

- Josh Becker,
The Guardian Life Insurance Company of America

"Through the ages, storytelling has preserved wisdom and made it available to those who want to hear and learn. In Be the First Believer, Ed Deutschlander, compiles many timeless gems along with his own original advice to instill important lessons in leadership. Every reader, no matter where they are in their career, will benefit from Ed's perspective, insight and wisdom. He leads a Financial Services firm whose mantra is "Changing Lives Forever."

Through these lessons and his passion he can change the reader's lives for the better. It is ours to hear and take to heart in what he is sharing through the wealth of his personal experiences. We will be better leaders of ourselves, our families, our companies and our future when we take action based on these lessons."

- Gary H Schwartz, Franchise Field Vice President, Ameriprise Financial (retired)

"Facts tell, stories sell." If indeed, selling is about persuading and being convincing, you will be a "believer" in Ed's point of view by the end of this book. The use of storytelling to make a point is both interesting and effective. Ed's insights are a bit of "truth serum" in an often-cynical world."

- M. Michael Rooney, CFP, ChFC, CLU,
AXA Advisors, LLC

"Ed Deutschlander is a visionary and thought leader for the financial services industry, he is a mentor to many, and a role model for everyone interested in succeeding in life. His book, Be The First Believer, should be required reading for everyone that wishes for success, happiness, and fulfillment in their lives. Ed's must read book provides a collection of practical principles Ed has collected over a lifetime of experiences and you do not want to miss any of them ! You will learn to lead your life with vision and humility, how to control your effort and attitude, and most importantly, how to maximize the present circumstances you face. Use Ed's "Quick Hits "to learn to believe in yourself and others more deep-

ly. You will become a "First Believer" in yourself and those you have the privilege to lead."

- Rodney E. Thornton, CLU®, ChFC®
Regional Managing Director, Principal Financial Group®

"Ed Deutschlander is a friend and an inspiration. Be The First Believer is the summation of Ed's learnings on the principles of leadership and the art of living life successfully. His mastery of both comes from his belief in, love for and giving to others. This book is another example of his lifetime of giving. Read it and learn the lessons from a man that lives it every day – you too will be inspired."

- Kurt D. Jonson, President,
Pacific Capital Resource Group, Inc.

"Ed Deutschlander is one of the most accomplished leaders in the financial services business. What he has laid out in this book, based on his vast experience is a "go to" guide path for both new and experienced leaders. I expect to be reading it every year as a leadership annual checkup. I will also refer to it when I am feeling things are not going the way I expect them to go. Using it as a checklist will reveal any problems. It is all about eliminating limitations, one's own and the limitations of others by creating expectations."

- Paul Vignone, CLU ChFC LLM,
Penn Mutual Life Insurance Company

"I have had the privilege to call Ed Deutschlander "friend" for nearly twenty years and my friend hits a home run in Be the First Believer!! In this book Ed takes a lifetime of leadership lessons and in a winsome and compelling manner transfers them to you. Be prepared to be inspired and challenged as you read this book!"

- Terry S. Wold, ChFC, CLU, FIC, Managing Partner,
Thrivent Financial for Lutherans

"A must read for all high school coaches, athletes, administrators, and parents. It not only provides a great path to leadership, it also addresses values that range from responsibility to work ethic. This book can serve as a road map on how to live your life. These life skills are extremely valuable in the high school athletic arena as well as the administrative offices."

- Bob Ferraro, Founder & Chief Executive Officer, NHSCA

"Bull's eye! This book is right on target and nothing short of brilliant, insightful and inspiring. It is an outstanding guide and "must read" for anyone who wants to improve their leadership skills; regardless of age or industry. The practical advice provided is invaluable and offers an unparalleled opportunity to learn from one of the best leaders and role models in business today. Be the First Believer should be required reading for all aspiring leaders and leadership teams."

- Steven D. Earhart, CLU, ChFC, MSFS, CFP,
Managing Partner, Devon Financial Partners, LLC

"Ed Deutschlander's book serves an exclamation point on his selection as North Star's next CEO. His wisdom, attitude, determination, and character come screaming off the pages of this work, which will no doubt serve as a standard by which others are measured. Bravo, Ed!"

- Phillip C. Richards, CFP, CLU, RHU,
North Star Resource Group Chairman & CEO

"Ed embodies the definition and principal of Servant Leadership. He has spent his entire career serving others. He continually puts the needs of others before his own and never misses an opportunity to teach or lead by example. The wisdom contained in this book is timeless and a must read for any young person looking to become a better leader, person, or human being. It has been an honor to call Ed one of my dearest friends for over 20 years. I couldn't imagine a better person to have as a friend, or for you to have as a teacher and a guide."

- P. Shaun McDuffee, AEP, CLU, ChFC, CEPA
Senior Vice President*, Senior Partner*,
North Star Resource Group

"Be The First Believer is what our mentors, coaches, teachers and parents wish they could have share with us. Here is a unique opportunity for all leaders and future leaders, young and old to discover the insights, the wisdom and the mastery of storytelling of one of our country's most gifted leaders, Ed Deutschlander. Leadership is about making choices, however this is not a choice but a must read for all."

- Richard T. Cleary, President and Managing Partner,
The Partners Network

"This book is a collection of ideas which represent the way Ed Deutschlander lives his life. You will find that the ideas shared here will not only help you with every day leadership ideas but also inspire you to move to a higher level of leadership. Just as Ed has!"

- Jim Petersen MSM, MSFS, CFP®, CLF®, ChFC®, CLU®, Financial Advisor, Principal and District Advisor, Parent of First Command Financial Planning

"The book is outstanding guide for people who want to truly understand leadership whether in their professional or personal life. I am going to use your book in my mentoring with young prisoners who are preparing to return to society. This is an awesome tool to teach these men leadership."

- Timothy P. Murray CLU, ChFC, President, Priority Financial Group LLC

"Be the First Believer is by far one of the best resources I have ever read on personal and professional leadership! For over two decades, people have drawn on the experiences and insight of Ed Deutschlander as he has given unselfishly. Now he has provided a timeless gift to leaders in all walks of life through his firsthand inspirational anecdotes and real life experiences. A treasure trove of sticky, easy to recall nuggets that should be required reading for anyone who influences or leads others."

- Joey Davenport, Principal & Chief Development Officer, Hoopis Performance Network

"Regardless of your chosen profession, or level of experience, I am certain you will enjoy this book. It is thought-provoking and will unquestionably cause you to re-evaluate some of your attitudes and behaviors. I have known Ed Deutschlander for many years and he is both a trusted colleague and a good friend. However, he is also someone who inspires me greatly with his commitment to living a life of integrity, and for constantly demonstrating what an honor he believes it is to serve others. Congratulations to you for the choice you have made to read this book. You will be better off for it, and so will the people whom you choose to serve."

- John W. Dixon, President, Capitol Financial Partners

"You could go out and read the best books on leadership, management, and peak performance or you could just read Ed's book. He has encapsulated the essence of all these domains into a truly enjoyable read. You will want to keep it as a handy reference even after you've read it."

- Jeff Golan, Regional Managing Director,
The Principal Financial Group

"Be The First Believer has real world applications for anyone in a leadership role or for those who just want to get more out of life. The leadership lessons shared by Ed Deutschlander are relevant, well laid out and easy to apply to your own situation."

- Tony Jennison, Head Football Coach, Macalester College

"Ed Deutschlander is one of the most innovative and strategic thinkers of his generation. This book offers leadership and life principles that he has learned throughout his life. I always find my time with Ed inspiring and thought provoking – this book is an extension of what makes him unique and motivating."

- David R. Pasciak, CLU, ChFC, CRPC, President,
VantagePointe Financial Group

"This is a fabulous collection of timeless leadership principles that should be a staple in every library. Ed Deutschlander is one of the most important leaders in the financial services industry of this century. Ed's visionary leadership, people skills and grasp of things that are most important, set him in a class all by himself. You will find yourself going back to this gem of a book not only for the defined leadership principles but for Ed's anecdotal stories that give them life."

- J. Christopher Noonan, ChFC, CLU,
Divisional Executive Vice President, AXA Advisors

"For those of you that want to be successful in any endeavor and achieve fulfillment in your life, Edward Deutschlander's book is a must read. One of the ongoing themes of Ed's book is that you are in control of your destiny. You must believe that you are going to achieve your dreams and goals that you have. You are in control, no one else.

You alone control your own attitude and the amount of effort you extend in whatever you wish to accomplish. That effort can develop habits that may not be particularly easy or pleasant to do, but will bring about the success you unquestionably believe and know you will achieve. Read Ed's book to learn the details of how you can do this. Ed is a testament to achieving success with the principles expounded in the book, he believes, he lives it."

- Donald J. Schoeller, CLU, ChFC, Senior Vice President*

"Unlike many who preach, Ed's message is founded in real world experiences as a community, industry, and family leader. Anyone who aspires to be a leader of people to advance causes they believe in, they need to read, if not study, this book. Ed has accomplished a fantastic job on an elusive topic with concrete and insightful life enhancing concepts. His ability to incorporate multiple metaphors and examples we see in everyday life helped me find at least one that crystalized the message.

Leadership Principles should be required reading for young adults. It is as good a source as I have seen to help prepare them to form the right habits and mindset that life requires if you are going to fully embrace life's opportunities. Ed's commitment to a balanced life allowed him to share messages to help others enjoy the fruits of a healthy, balance life themselves. Ed shares 50 ideas all of which I fund value."

- Richard McCloskey

ACKNOWLEDGEMENTS

Ed Deutschlander

I first want to take a moment and thank my good friend Rich Campe. Without Rich I am unsure as to when this book would have been written. Rich provided the support, accountability and structure that I needed to get this onto paper and into a format that hopefully will inspire and assist many. Thank you Rich for making one of my dreams come true writing this book. I also want to thank Lauren Barker. Lauren is a very talented college student that we hired as an intern to assist with some of this project. Rich and I made it a point to identify talented up and coming writers that we could enlist their help in some of the book as we want to help develop the future in whatever way possible. By giving talented young people like Lauren opportunities we know we are playing a part in shaping the future.

To mention everyone that has played a part in my life that has contributed to this collection of lessons is not possible. With that I will try my best to honor as many as I can.

To my childhood friends in Chicago, you are remembered.

To my high school teammates, thanks for accepting me into a new community.

To my college teammates, thank you for your lifelong friendship, memories and lessons both on and off the field.

To my study group members, your support and friendship means the world.

To GAMA, the GAMA Foundation, NAIFA, MDRT, LIMRA and The American College - our cause is noble and I admire the work you all do on behalf of our industry.

To Securian, thank you for the support and on-going encouragement

To all of the advisors and team members at North Star, I cannot imagine my life without North Star Resource Group.

To Phil Richards, thank you for expecting greatness from me

To my Family, words fail.

This book is dedicated in loving memory of those who are no longer with us in person but with us in spirit as you made a difference. Edward and Harriet Deutschlander, George and Anna Aird, Dori Green. The people who have made and given retreats at Demontreville retreat house, Sheri Schoeller, Dave Nelson, Jim Krueger, Norb Winter, Brian Early and my brother in Christ--- Scott Richards.

ACKNOWLEDGEMENTS
RICH CAMPE

I'd like to thank my friend, co-author and top leader Ed Deutschlander for the opportunity to partner in such a great adventure as ***Be The First Believer***. Your leadership insights have been a true gift for myself and countless others.

Hannah Davis for editing, layout and formatting early on and Deborah Hawkins for getting us in the end zone.

Great lifelong friends through thick and thin... Leonard Wheeler, Brian Chapman, Anita Grund, Glen Viditz-Ward, Haywood "The Wood" Thompson, Douglas Graham "Doggie", Ken Klug "Shrek", Billy Irby "Firby", HR Goff, Matt and Shelly Yoder, Craig Tarmontano, HR Goff, Jay Hakim, Jim Pollitt, Eddy Cadiz, Fernando Villanueva, John DeTolve, Tim Herbord and Bob Kunkel

Amazing business partners, associates and friends for always raising the bar and deciphering the many great ideas into action... Debbie Buckley, Michael Vines, Mike Agugliaro, Jamie Croland, Jim Schlesinger, John Lucas and Machen McDonald. Thanks for always raising the bar!

My College business professor Dr. Gary Ernst. Thanks for believing in me!

My Martial Arts Instructor Head Instructor Mark Ambrogio. Thanks for pushing me to the limits!

Our Publisher Jamie Morrison and all our friends at Believers Press. Your dedication and commitment are inspirational and commended. Thank You!

The Very Talented clients who have become great Friends while always reaching for the best within themselves and others "well…at least the majority of the time.. LOL". Scott Meyerson, Jon Massey, Tom Mingone, Donna Nadler, Tim Maguire, David Karr, Chris Strivieri, Andrew Avellan, Jonathan Marsh, Edwin Soto Quinones, Alex Dergalis, Mark Johnson, William D. "Bo" Keltner and the countless others that I've had the privilege to partner with along the way. Thank You from the bottom of my heart!

The most Amazing sister a brother could ever ask for… Shannon you are my "Rock." My Brother in Law "BBF" for always toeing the line and holding the course. My kids Camden and Lawson for so much love and patience. My dad Dave Campe for always playing full out till his final days when he passed away from his battle with cancer on June 29, 2009. My mom for her never ending love, compassion and leadership example in continuing to win the cancer challenge… Love you Momacita!

PREFACE

By Walter Bond

As I gather myself to write a preface that is real and authentic, I want to be careful to make sure I capture the essence of not only this book but who Rich Campe and Ed Deutschlander are as people.

I have been speaking professionally for the past thirteen years and have received many awards along this prosperous and rewarding journey. I am a Certified Speaking Professional (CSP), which there are only 600 worldwide, have been voted "speaker of the year" by Minnesota Meetings & Events and one publication listed me as a top 5 speaker on motivation. Simply put, God himself has placed a precious gift inside of me and God has also opened up doors for me to impact crowds as large as 16,000 people.

In order for me to be a professional speaker of any significance I had to become my own first believer. I learned this lesson long before I even became a motivational speaker. In a previous life I graced the hardwood as an NBA athlete playing with the Utah Jazz, Dallas Mavericks and Detroit Pistons. Before I even knew Rich or Ed, the principles that are shared in this book were being displayed and discovered on my journey to the NBA in my own life. While in the NBA I had legendary teammates like Karl Malone, John Stockton and Coach Jerry Sloan who was a great coach, why? Glad you asked, because he was a great leader of men.

Not to mention that I host my own reality show on the Food Network called "Giving You the Business" where I work closely with some of the most dynamic leaders in the franchise world and award a franchise to one of their top employees for being excellent and winning a competition they don't even know they are competing for. These employees are caught being good, doing the right thing when nobody is looking or at least they think.

I say all of that to say this, I was asked to write this preface because I have "been there" and "done that." Most importantly I have been around some great people that have achieved extraordinary success. So, that brings me to Rich and Ed. I know when people have what I call the "It" factor. Something about them sets them apart from the crowd, and there is much more power when you get two people together that have the "It" factor like Rich and Ed have done with this book. Magic is taboo to some, but when these two connect, nothing but magic can happen for lack of a better term.

I met Rich Campe at one of my many seminars. We were in North Carolina and we were both on the same program for Allianz. I followed his powerful message and before he could retreat back to his hotel room he stuck around long enough to hear me, and that day a friendship was born. We found out that we were both from Chicago, born on the same day at the same hospital. Yes, ladies and gentlemen "fate" brought us together as men of faith and men committed to helping others live their dream. I have known Rich to be sincere, caring and SMART! A good dude, as we would say in Chicago in my part of town. Rich Campe is my dawg!

I have really valued and enjoyed our friendship and the experience of co-authoring a book with him myself; "The Off-Season for Financial Advisors." During that process I saw his attention to detail, work ethic and professional abilities that are second to none. I know Rich personally and have done a major project with him and he is the real deal. Rich even came to Minnesota for a weekend and tailgated with me at a Gopher game. If you tailgate with me, you are a friend for life.

The funny thing is that we launched our book at GAMA, which is a watering hole for some of the top leaders and trend setters in the financial services industry. This is where Rich introduced me to Ed. I was there to be the keynote speaker, man of the hour - that dude for a day. As Rich introduced Ed, he gave him so much respect as he briefed me on who Ed was, I thought he should have been the one giving the keynote that day… not me. As Ed and I began to connect in the lobby of the crowded hotel, fans walked by saying "hi" to Ed and not to me. I was like, who is this dude? I need to know him, come to find out we have a lot in common. We both lived in Minneapolis, we had kids about the same age and we both had been successful in sports and business. Ed was easy to connect with and had an intensity that is consistent with being a football player. A football player understands leverage, stamina and positioning. Those football dudes are a different breed. They are focused, committed and play through pain, blood, sweat and tears. Football players know how to get it and have a look in their eyes that will make you yell "uncle."

After a brief meeting with Ed that night and a couple future meetings with him back in Minnesota, I now know for myself why Rich thinks so highly of Ed. He is a relentless and tireless worker, they both are, and I know they poured their hearts and souls into this book. So here we are, two guys with the "It" factor coming together to make magic together.

I have been around great people all my life, in sports, business and industry. I attended my father Willie Bond's elementary and high schools in Chicago, so I saw the "It" factor close up at a young age by just watching my dad. I have seen men and women with the "It" factor for a long time. Simply put, Rich & Ed have the "It" factor and that will become obvious as you enjoy the powerful expression of their greatness. I hope you find this book insightful, powerful and life-changing as you become your first believer.

TABLE OF CONTENTS

INTRODUCTION: THINKING ABOUT THINKING

PART 1: KNOWING YOURSELF

PART 2: MENTAL PREPARATION (ATTITUDE)

PART 3: SOUND DECISION MAKING (EFFORT)

PART 4: SHARP SKILLS

PART 5: LEADING WITH VISION AND HUMILITY

PART 6: QUICK HITS

INTRODUCTION

By Rich Campe

What comes first? The action, result or the thinking? All action must start with a thought – the thinking. Just as all life starts with a seed, all actions and results start with a thought.

I had the unique opportunity to meet Ed Deutschlander several years ago at GAMA (General Agents and Managers Association) and then later that year at MDRT (Million Dollar Round Table). It was as if we were kindred spirits from the first time we connected.

Ed and I connected at several other conferences and meetings from that initial time that built our relationship and calling to share more together. When Ed approached me with the idea to write a book together it was a resounding "Yes... of Course." Because of my background in coaching and knowing that the answers are in the questions and knowing Ed had leadership golden nuggets ready to be shared with the world, we began the adventure. With each moment we spent together I felt like a detective picking up gold, silver and precious gems with every conversation. The following pages include the precious metals that we harnessed into this book called ***Be The First Believer.***

It has been a great privilege and an honor working with Ed, an industry icon and friend, to discover and capture the following information in this book – the seeds of great thinkers. Our prayer is that the following seeds within ***Be The First Believer*** capture your thinking muscles and inspire you to think bigger, bolder and brighter. We also pray that you take these thinking seeds and water them to achieve extraordinary new levels of awareness, leadership and success.

A journey of a thousand miles starts with a first step and no matter your current location on your journey; whether it be at the top of your game or just getting started ***Be The First Believer*** is a great way to sharpen your thinking seeds of greatness.

As a Free gift to you we would like to offer the first of many challenges in this book. We're offering you the opportunity to take MindScan Assessment. Your personalized MindScan profile will help you create a deeper awareness of yourself.

The foundation for MindScan is based upon the ground-breaking work of Dr. Robert S. Hartman. He created a method that actually measures how people think, and identifies their strengths and uniqueness; which earned him a Nobel Prize nomination.

His legacy has been to leave with us an instrument that is more powerful and unlike any other process on the market today because it actually measures the elements so critical to success in today's environment. It does not place you into labeled groups, rather it treats you individually. The first step is to understand how you think; the second step is to be able to utilize the power of the information. Applied correctly, this profile should have a major impact on you personally and your career.

You can take the MindScan Profile for Free ($500 value) with the following link: www.proadvisorcoach.com/bethefirstbeliever. Again, this is our gift to you and it will only take 20 minutes or less. Thank you.

Be The First Believer

A Collection Of Leadership Lessons For Life

Ed Deutschlander and Rich Campe

CHAPTER 1:
Be The First Believer

"You have to be the first believer." This was the answer the legendary coach Jim Valvano gave when the rumor surfaced about his team spending their entire first practice of the season dedicated to the ritual of cutting down the nets, pretending they just won the national championship. There were no basketballs at that first practice, there were no whistles. What was there was a ladder, a pair of golden scissors and a vision. A vision that one day all of those players would not be practicing this exercise but rather living it. It seems rather childish that a Division 1 basketball program would be participating in such antics. The interesting part was that no one was laughing as Jim Valvano spent a lot of time in March of 1983 in front of the camera giving interviews. He was watched by millions as his North Carolina State Wolfpack went on to what many would claim to be the greatest upset ever in college sports. His team did indeed cut down the nets, winning the NCAA Division 1 Basketball Championship.

Jim Valvano understood what a leader's responsibility is - *to lead*. To lead to a desired outcome, result, destination, or goal. For that to happen, someone needs to be the very first believer that something can be done and accomplished. If it is not the leader, then who else can it be? The interesting part is that every single one of us is a leader. At the very least we are the leader of our lives. We need to be the first believer in ourselves and for the goals, aspirations and the life we envision.

This book is designed to help one become a better leader, regardless of their path, lot or journey in life. From the student-athlete, to the parent, teacher, coach, business owner or financial advisor, all of us need to lead and will be counted on to lead at numerous points as we rotate around the sun together.

The contents of this book are a series of leadership and life principles that I have collected over my lifetime. Some are my own discoveries, many I learned from others, some whom I have never met yet they impacted me and the direction of my life. What I try to do when I learn of one of these principles, is to capture it in a sound-bite or a headline that is easy to remember. My objective is to take perhaps a complex lesson and make it something that is digestible and can be recalled quickly from memory.

The genesis of this book started years ago. I was asked to give a presentation on leadership (having some small success in my professional life the request was made of me to share what I attributed my success to). This request forced me to reflect and I soon realized that a host of lessons learned, and frequently acted upon, served as one of the main drivers of my accomplishments. After the presentation I reflected even further and continued writing down all the lessons learned from my childhood, student-athlete days in college, family life and career. The list still continues to grow to this day and over 100 lessons are now captured on that list. This book will focus on the foundational lessons of that list. Now back to Jim Valvano.

Jim Valvano said something in one brief interview which changed my life. With the statement, "you have to be the first believer", the light bulb went on for me. It all starts with me. If I am to accomplish anything, become anything, impact or change anything, I must understand that I have to believe first and foremost. The old adage of "believe and achieve" and "if it is to be it is up to me" is completely captured in this simple yet profound statement. Over the years as I have reviewed my list, I am always surprised how being the first believer is the prerequisite to almost every principle on the list. Jim Valvano walked his talk. He was the first believer that his team could win a national title. As he was losing his fight with cancer he still believed he could beat the odds. Jim Valvano was the first believer that his mess could be his message and that he believed he could begin something that could perhaps one day eradicate cancer from this earth. With the help of ESPN the Jimmy V. Foundation was started which has raised over 100 million dollars for cancer research. Thousands of lives have been saved because he was the first believer!

All of us need to be the first believer in something. That something is our very own future. What do you want? How do you want to be remembered? What legacy will you leave? It all starts with being the first believer.

It is serendipitous that this morning on a flight to Phoenix I decided to write the opening chapter of this book. My daughter Ashley, a college student-athlete, scholarship Lacrosse player, responded to an email in which I was asking her the dates of the National tournament her team just qualified for. Here is the email exchange:

On Mar 28, 2013, at 2:37 PM, "Deutschlander, Ed" <ed@northstarfinancial.com> wrote:

Ashley

Please give me OFFICIAL dates of the NWLL Nationals so I can look into attending the games. I need the dates you play or most likely will be playing.

Love DAD

Hey Dad,

We will have our first game on Thursday the 18th and the last game would be Sunday the 21st if we make it that far!

Love you
Ash

Sent from my iPhone

You will
Be the first believer

Love
DAD

Whether or not my daughter's team wins the National Championship is still an unknown. However in a phone conversation with her mother late that day, she told her Mom that they were going to win the national title. I am going to take some credit that the email exchange reminded her of what I have shared with her throughout her entire life - BELIEVE.

If there is one takeaway from this book I hope it is you learn to believe in yourself and others more deeply. Everyone needs someone in their life to expect greatness from them. You can be that one for many and in doing so you will see how many will expect greatness from you.

So as we journey through this book together my wish for you is that you benefit from these lessons and become the first believer in your own one, God given life and be the first believer in those you have the privilege of leading.

God Bless
Ed Deutschlander

CHAPTER 2:
Watch Your A&E

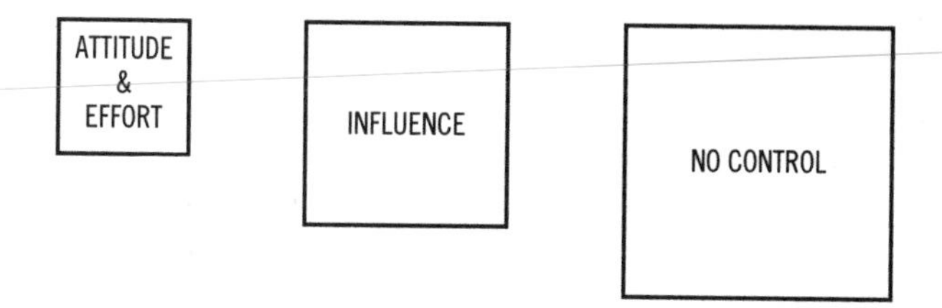

If you look at some of the most successful people in the world, you will discover that they are very disciplined in their ability to always monitor their Attitude and their Effort, or A & E. These people are masters at always monitoring and adjusting to whatever degree necessary in their attitude and effort.

We truly believe that in life, there are two things that you have complete control over. First, you have complete control over your attitude toward whatever it is that you are pursuing. Second, you have complete control over the effort you are putting forth on a daily basis toward endeavors you have chosen to spend your time and energy on.

At North Star Resource Group, we do an exercise where we have people draw a small box. Inside that box, they write, "Attitude and Effort." That first box depicts what they have control over, at all times and that is irrefutable. Other people can influence your attitude and effort, of course, but you are the one who is in complete control of these two important things.

Next, we have people draw another slightly larger box. In that box, we have them write the word "Influence." This demonstrates that there are a number of things in life that we have influence over - not complete control, but influence. For instance, in the business world, and specifically as a financial advisor, you have influence over whether the prospect eventually decides to work with you. You do not have complete control; it is the prospect who determines whether they agrees with your conclusions, your strategies, your recommendations, your products, and your services. The prospect will decide if they work with you, so the prospect has ultimate control in that situation, but, by all means, you do have an influence.

Lastly, we have people draw an even larger box, and inside that box we have them write "No Control." This represents most things in life that, frankly, we don't have any control over. We have complete control over our attitude and effort; we have an influence over many things, but the majority of things in this world are beyond our control. The problem is that we focus our precious time and energy on the things we have no control over instead of focusing on what we have influence or complete control over.

If you look at the most successful people in the world, you will find that they have ways of constantly adjusting their attitude to keep it positive and make sure it's on the right track. They have ways of making sure that the effort they are putting forth in their daily activities is at the appropriate level for them to meet their goals.

Everyone is going to have obstacles and challenges and times when their attitude might wane and their effort might dissipate, but that's OK. That's human. We all have to focus and reengage and monitor our attitude and our effort to make sure they are appropriate to complete our tasks and to achieve our goals.

CHAPTER 3:

Big Trophy Day

The people that are good at managing their Attitude and Effort have gone through some difficult times, such as bankruptcy, divorce, or the death of a family member. Through all of that, these people are still able to manage their Attitude and Effort. So how do you do it when things get tough? Anybody can manage their Attitude and Effort when life is going well, but when things get hard, how do we manage our A & E?

This moves into our next key principle, which I call "Big Trophy Day." Big Trophy Day is based on my personal story, but before I tell it, I will set the stage. To keep your attitude and effort on the right track, you first need to establish your "Why." What is it you are trying to accomplish? What is so important to you that you're waking up every day? What is your mission? What is your goal? What is your objective? All of these terms are somewhat synonymous with one another, but I like to use the word "Why" specifically because it gets to the heart of the matter. Why are you doing this? Why do you exist? Why are you willing to tolerate short term sacrifices? Why are you willing to persist in the face of adversity? In other words, what is your "Why?"

Everyone's "Why" is different; there is no right "Why" and there is no wrong "Why." Everyone has to take the time to decide what their "Why" is. You have to ask yourself why you are pursuing something and why that pursuit is a priority for you. Once that is established, you can overcome any "How." When you have a strong enough "Why", you can overcome any "How" - any situation, any setback, any obstacle, any adversity, because your Why is so strong. Viktor Frankl said it best in his wonderful gift to the world, the book ***Man's Search for Meaning...*** "*A man who becomes conscious of the responsibility he bears toward a human being who affectionately waits for him, or to an unfinished work, will never be able to throw away his life*". He knows the *why* of his existence, and will be able to bear almost any *how*.

The challenge is that most people never make that connection. They do not take enough time to reflect on their priorities. They never truly establish their "*Why.*" They never ask themselves, why is this so important to me?

The personal story I am going to share is about my son, who is now 17 years old. When he was 6 years old, he had been taking karate lessons for a year and his karate instructor suggested that he go to a karate tournament. As excited parents, we immediately signed him up for his first ever karate tournament. On the day of the event, my wife and I went to the arena and watched our son compete. After waiting for a long time, he finally got in the ring.

Unfortunately, the fight was over before it began. It lasted maybe fifteen-seconds, his opponent scored points very quickly, and just like that, it was over. Because they encourage participation today, everyone was a winner. So my son got a participation trophy medal for participating. But he saw what the winner of the tournament received, a big trophy.

When we were driving home, my son said, "Mom, Dad, did you see that the winner of the tournament got one of those big trophies?"

Yes, we did.

"Well, you know what? I'm gonna win one of those trophies."

Being encouraging parents, my wife and I told him, absolutely, Jake. Keep working hard, stay focused, and that will happen. It's not 'if,' it's 'when.'

When Jake returned to his karate lessons, he was much more engaged. His instructor told my wife, "Jake's more focused in practice. He's more engaged." Sure enough, it was because he had found his "Why." His "Why" was one of those big trophies.

A couple of months later, another tournament rolled around. Jake signed up again, and this time he was much more excited and enthusiastic about the tournament. The Saturday morning of the tournament, I went to wake him up bright and early.

"Hey, Jake! Wake up, Bud! Do you know what today is?" I said, fishing for a sense of where he was mentally.

"Yeah, Dad!" he said. "Today's Big Trophy Day!"

This caught me off guard and took me a minute to process. Then it occurred to me, Jake thinks he's going to win the big trophy today. I was so excited for him and his positive attitude. I had just been hoping he would say it was the day of the karate tournament. His response that it was "Big Trophy Day" told me that he was already very focused.

By 2:00 that afternoon, Jake was proudly holding 2 big trophies. He had won 1st place in form and 1st place in sparring for his age group and belt level. I thought, is there something special about this kid besides the fact that he's my son? No.

This is how we are hardwired. As humans, we are goal-thinking, striving creatures and when we have a goal, it is amazing what happens. I learned this from a six-year-old. For him, it was simple. He wanted a big trophy, and he found a way to get it.

So now I encourage people to answer this question, what is your Big Trophy Day, or, what is your "Why?" Why are you willing to go through some of the sacrifices or heartache or adversity? It is all about making sure that you have the right attitude and that you put forth the best effort possible.

To answer the question that began this chapter, yes, we are going to get off track. That is inevitable. Life happens. What is going to keep us on track and allow us to stay focused is knowing what our "Why" is and having our own personal Big Trophy Day.

9:00 AM
WARMING UP TO COMPETE

2:00 PM
1ST PLACE IN BOTH FORM AND SPARRING

NOW THAT IS A BIG TROPHY!!

CHAPTER 4:
WAYB
Who Are You Becoming? Who Are You Being?

Wherever you are, be there. To me, the definition of success is the person who is waking up every day, who lives by a set of values, who has a goal, an objective, and a why in their life that they are trying to accomplish. This person is putting forth the most effort and energy possible to get there. Whether they are a teacher, coach, doctor, lawyer, engineer, artist, financial advisor, working in a nonprofit sector, or running a business. It doesn't matter if they make $25,000 a year or $25,000,000 a year. Success is not about titles or income or net worth. Interestingly, individuals are often rewarded with high net worth, high incomes, and a great deal of responsibility. Sometimes they are even rewarded with titles, but that is an ancillary benefit of the principles we are talking about.

It's important for us to look to the future; people have to focus on the future when thinking about their goals, but it is important not to neglect the present. The most successful people in the world have the ability to maximize their current situation. The past is over. Successful people use the past as a lesson. They look toward the future because that is what gives them hope and helps them work through adversity. But they are extremely good at focusing on the present. Wherever you are, be there.

Let's use the example of a successful businesswoman. She is having a conversation with her key people. She is not thinking about the board meeting that is happening in a week or her son who failed his geometry test. At the moment, all of her energy is focused on the issues at hand with that key conversation with that key employee. The employee is the center of her attention. When she is with her family, she is not thinking about meetings or to-do lists for the next day. She is not replaying the conversation she had at the workplace or on the golf course earlier that day. She is engaged and focused on her relationships at home; her children and her spouse. She understands the importance of maximizing the present - Wherever you are, be there.

When you maximize the present, you will be amazed by the lessons that you learn or the things you observe. More important, when you maximize the present, it allows the people around you to see that you care, and when people see that you care, they will do just about anything in the world for you or with you.

Too often, we do not maximize today because we are too busy focusing on the should've, would've, could've of two hours ago, or two weeks ago, or two years ago. Or, we are too busy thinking, "OK, I have to do this, that, this and that" instead of maximizing today.

So how do you get to a place where you can maximize today? What are the steps?

It starts with conditioning; it is like exercise or working a muscle. It does not occur overnight. Often times, people get discouraged because they want instant results.

Today, we live in a world where instant gratification is so prevalent. Whatever it is you want, you name it, and you can have it now – that is what the world and media try to drill in our heads. We know better, we know that discipline and consistent effort win the day and that shines through with what we know as delayed gratification. When it comes to your ability to maximize the present, the discipline to stay focused on the task and the people at hand, this will provide you observations and experiences that you will cherish for a lifetime.

PART 2:

Mental Preparation (Attitude)

CHAPTER 5:
Success Is a Matter of 18 Inches

In humans, the average space between the top of the brain and the center of the heart is 18 inches. The head and the heart are the 2 things that you have to connect to be really successful. The most successful people in the world have been able to make this connection. These people certainly have the mental capacity for their pursuits, and they also might have a gift or affinity toward their pursuits, but they also have an incredible passion. They truly love what they are doing. They have effectively connected the head and the heart.

Many people have a God given talent or a knack for a certain thing. For example, Malcolm Gladwell shares in his incredible book ***Outliers*** the story of Chris Langan. Who is Chris Langan? That is exactly the point. Chris Langan is documented as having the highest I.Q. on the planet, but yet he has contributed virtually nothing to society. The reasons are many, bad breaks, attitude, and many other setbacks listed in the book. I agree with Gladwell, but I also believe a major contributor to the lack of impact and success by Langan is that he never connected his head to his heart.

Then there are those individuals all over the world who may not have the most talent - they're not the smartest, they're not the fastest, they're not the biggest, they're not the brightest -and yet they go on to accomplish tremendous feats. That is because they have connected the head and the heart. They have put their mind and their passion together and done amazing things.

A great example of this is Larry Bird. Bird was not the greatest athlete when he started playing, but he became one of the greatest basketball players of all time because he loved the game. He knew he had to work harder than his competitors because they were more athletically gifted than he was. Bird did not let his stronger competitors stand in the way of his goal. Larry Bird positively connected the head and the heart.

In order to connect the head to the heart one must identify their "why." The "why" is the heart of the head and heart equation. The head is the "what" of the head and the heart equation. Another way of looking at it is asking the question, "what is your goal and why is it the goal?" When one clearly identifies a goal and knows the deep rooted meaning of why the goal is important to them, the head and heart becomes connected and the power behind that connection will thrust them towards reaching the goal in a manner they never thought possible.

CHAPTER 6:
Always Be a Little Bit Out of Control

I once saw Mario Andretti, the world class Hall of Fame race car driver, give an interview. They asked him what he attributed his illustrious professional sports career to. Andretti responded, "The reason I'm such a successful race car driver is that whenever I felt like I had complete control over the race car, I knew I was not going fast enough. My goal was to always be a little bit out of control. When I felt just a bit out of control, I had a chance to win the race. If not, I knew others would pass me up."

I found Andretti's response to be profound. His words resonated with me, because this idea does not just apply to race car driving. It's about life. Often, we get caught up in the idea that we have to have everything under control. So, we work hard until we get to a point where we can take a deep breath and relax, because everything is under control. I'm not saying that this is a bad thing, but when you get to that point, you're probably not pushing yourself hard enough.

You always want to be a little bit out of control. That's how you should feel. When you're at your best, when you're really excelling, when you're really getting things done, life is a little hectic and stressful. You have white knuckles when you look down at the steering wheel, but that is not a bad thing. What we can learn from Mario Andretti is that pushing yourself is a good thing. It's great to be taking on lots of responsibility, serving a lot of people, and doing a lot of good things.

Years ago while on a religious retreat I came across a lesson from St. Francis of Assisi. While ministering, St. Francis was approached by a young priest who asked if he could accompany him for the day as he wanted to learn all he could from his mentor. St. Francis was happy and honored to accommodate the request. Throughout the day they went to several villages and towns in Italy where they tended to the sick and served food to the hungry, mostly done in silence. After the long and arduous day, the young priest was disappointed in that very little was said as he was expecting great words of wisdom to be spoken on the ministering trip. He asked St. Francis if he felt any of those they served learned anything of God. St. Francis responded, "It is not in what we say but in our actions and what we do. We did nothing but minister today; they saw the hand of God. While we have time, let us do good."

Reading the story reminded me of all the good work, action and impact all of us have the potential of doing each day. However it is going to require that we are demanding of ourselves and push ourselves in the very same way Mario Andretti pushed himself in that race car. This puts us in a state of being a little out of control. Being a little bit out of control inherently has a message of urgency in it. That sense of urgency is heard in St. Francis message, "while we have the time", as one day it will end. One needs to have the sense of urgency to win the race. Adopting a mindset of being a little out of control brings urgency and impact to everything one does.

When everything is under control and you can relax a little, it's not necessarily a bad thing, but you're probably not using all of your talents as best as you could if you felt a little bit of pressure. Keeping things at a very high level of acceleration is what will push you to make strides. Everyone has experienced this. When you look back, it is often the times that you were a little stressed where you accomplished the most as well.

Another example of this idea is the way a kite flies. To stay in the air, the wind has to be constantly pushing against the kite. It's the constant tension that causes the kite to fly. Tension is not always a bad thing. In many cases, tension is what fuels success.

CHAPTER 7:
Pressure vs. Stress

It is important to understand the difference between pressure and stress. Pressure is inevitable. We live in a world that is full of all kinds of pressure. It is something that is constantly surrounding us. You are going to have pressure in your personal life as well as in your professional responsibilities.

Consequently, stress is what you experience when you are not prepared for pressure. So to avoid stress, we have to train our minds to embrace pressure.

In 2008, Billie Jean King wrote a wonderful book titled ***Pressure is a Privilege***. Pressure is just that - a privilege. Think about it. When you're in pressure situations, you're doing something special. When you're under pressure, you're doing something important. Something that matters.

Let's look at a professional athlete. The game is on the line and she is trying to make the winning free throw. That's special. To get to that point, she first made the team, worked hard to become a starter, and kept that position. Now, her teammates are relying on her, like they have countless times before. To get to that spot is a privilege.

For another example, take a businessman who is preparing to give a presentation to a Board of Directors. Before this point, he had to get the job and excel at his position. His superiors have given him a large amount of responsibility, and now, someone has asked him to give a presentation to the board. This means that his superiors trust him enough to put together a brilliant presentation and represent the company. He is under pressure, but it is a very positive pressure. Many people never get the opportunity to experience such pressures.

If you are not experiencing pressure in your life, chances are you are not doing enough. Pressure is something you feel when you are active and engaged. Pressure is a privilege; it's a good thing. Take advantage of pressure.

The trick we have to learn is preparing for pressure. When we are not prepared for pressure, we experience stress. Perhaps you're a student, going in to take an exam. You may feel stressed out because you haven't mastered all the material. The pressure of the exam is always going to be there. If you study, however, you do not experience stress. Instead, you embrace the exam; you even get a little excited about it, because you know you're going to do really well. You're prepared.

We have all experienced pressure and stress. Sometimes, we're prepared for the pressure of an important situation. Other times, we aren't, and we experience stress. So how do we keep our lives from spinning out of control? Preparation.

To begin preparing for situations that lie ahead of us, we have to focus on what we can control. We control our attitude and effort. Effort is how you prepare for something. What you put into a situation is what you will get out of it. Successful people prepare by putting lots of effort into their tasks, and they are rewarded for their effort. These successful people embrace pressure. They believe that pressure is a privilege. They look for pressure situations. They want to be right there. Because these people put forth the time, energy, dedication, and effort to prepare for pressure situations they do not become overwhelmed.

You want to find yourself in pressure situations, because that tells you that you're doing something right. What you want to avoid is stress.

Sometimes, you can be prepared and not achieve the result you wanted. That happens. It's life. Sometimes you work hard and take time to prepare, but things just do not go your way. You can't let that depress you, because deep down you know that you worked hard. You laid it all out on the line. The greatest feeling in the world is when you have put forth as much effort as possible. It feels even better when you're victorious. There will be times when you put forth as much effort as possible, when you really lay it all out on the field and you're not victorious, but it still feels good to put forth that effort. Deep down, you know you did all right, because you put forth as much effort as you could have.

In college, there were times when I got an A in a class and it wasn't very meaningful because the course wasn't very challenging. Then there were times when I got a C in a class and I felt good about that C because I worked hard - I laid it all out on the line. Sometimes, I learned more in those classes where I got C's instead of the classes where I got A's. The difference was the effort that I put forth.

CHAPTER 8:
Victory in Defeat, Defeat in Victory

Our world teaches us that winning is good and losing is bad. I would argue that you shouldn't think that way. Winning and getting positive results is great, but there is something deeper in competing. Competition is everywhere in life. Victory in defeat is when you learn from defeat. You might not win the game, you might not get an A in the class, you might not get the job, and you might not get the client. Victory in defeat happens when you give everything you have, when you make an all-out effort and you can reflect on what happened. You learn a lesson and you figure out how to improve.

So sometimes when you lose, you really win. You learn from your mistakes and analyze what went wrong in a way that you probably would not do if you had won. You have reflected and made a discovery, which will only help you in the long run.

Sometimes in victory, there is defeat. A lot of times when we win, we don't go into that reflective mode. We don't stop to think about what we may have done wrong or what we could have done better. We don't realize that we may have just gotten lucky. We usually just think, OK, we won. Let's celebrate and move on to the next game, the next task.

The very best, most successful people go back and review even after they have won. They look at film, review notes, or replay conversations with their clients. They look at what they could improve upon. Many times, winning is about luck, but luck is unpredictable. What is predictable is effort. Therefore, a good question to ask ourselves after a victory is: "Did we put forth our best effort?" Hopefully, the answer to that question is yes, but if we didn't put forth our best effort, we should ask "why not?" and "how can we fix that?"

Next, we have to look at what lessons we might have learned and how we can improve. All too often, that doesn't happen, which leads to defeat in victory. Do not let the scoreboard tell the whole story.

I will end this chapter with a few examples of the totality of victory and defeat. In the 1990's I remember seeing a commercial that featured Michael Jordan, arguably the greatest basketball player to ever grace the NBA courts. In the commercial Michael Jordan recites the following:

"I've missed 9,000 shots in my career."

"I've lost almost 3,000 games."

"26 times, I've been trusted with the ball to take the game winning shot."

"And missed."

"I've failed over and over and over again in my life."

"And that is why I succeed."

VICTORY IN DEFEAT

If you ever want to be inspired it won't take more than 4 minutes. I would highly recommend that you go to YouTube and watch the battle between Wendy Ingraham and Sian Welch that occurred in the 1997 Ironman World Championships. Words do not do justice in describing what one witnesses when they watch "The Crawl". After 140 miles of intense competition these women literally gave everything they had to finish 4th and 5th in the world respectively. Even though both of these women did not finish 1st that day, one will see from this emotional finish that both of these women experienced victory in defeat.

VICTORY IN DEFEAT

And lastly perhaps the most powerful example ever left on this earth of victory in defeat, is the symbol of Christianity. Jesus' death on the cross is the ultimate victory for Christians around the world. No cross, no crown.

CHAPTER 9:
Deserve to Win Mentality

Deserve to Win Mentality is the attitude that we have to bring to the table whenever we are trying to accomplish our goals or objectives. Earlier we touched on watching your attitude and your effort. This principle falls under that in a way. When you put forth effort, when you work very hard at something, when you give it your all, you put forth blood, sweat, and tears. This allows you to walk into a situation - whether it is an athletic event, the test you are taking, or the big presentation you are giving to a client - you have the mindset of; "I deserve to win and the reason I deserve to win is because I have prepared for this. I have prepared more than my opponent, more than the competition. I have prepared enough where this is my game to win."

That mindset is so important because we are our own worst enemy. Often, the reason we don't hit our goal or objective is because we allow a little bit of doubt to creep into our mind. We continually ask ourselves, "Am I good enough? Am I ready? Did I prepare well enough?" If you work really hard, your effort can eliminate those doubts. When those doubts creep in, you can convince yourself that you do deserve to win because you have worked so hard toward your goal.

A great example in the coaching world is Rick Patino. He fostered a deserve to win mentality on his basketball teams. In his book, ***Success is a Choice*** he talked about how he convinced his basketball players that they worked harder than any other team in America. He did this by having his team practice 15 minutes longer than most teams did and those 15 minutes added up during the course of the season. Once, when the game was on the line, Patino took a time out and brought his team together. There were 30 seconds left on the clock and his team was down by one point. Patino reminded his players that they deserved to win because they worked harder than the other team and they deserved it. They deserved it more than their opponents did. Patino told his players to go out onto the court and make sure they got what they deserved. Sure enough, this reminder spurred the team on and gave them the right frame of mind. The lesson to take away from this story is that we control our attitude in this world. We control our effort.

Basically, you have to create the proper mindset. You have to convince yourself that you deserve to achieve your goal. You have to remind yourself that you worked hard, you put in the extra hours at work and you went the extra mile so you deserve to win.

A friend of mine is very successful in the financial services industry. He grew up in a very wealthy household, and his father was very successful. His father told all of his children that they needed to go blaze their own trail in the world and make their own mark. He also told them not to count on him for an inheritance because his money would all be left to charity. He said, "I'm doing this for your own good in life because if I don't you will have that entitlement mentality." So they worked hard for their whole lives. My friend went on to be very successful in the financial services industry. One of his siblings went on to become very successful in medicine and the others in their various pursuits – they all went on and did very well. Eventually, their father's health was ailing, and so they all went back home to spend time with him.

"Hey Dad," one of them said, "We have all been successful in our own right. We are putting your final affairs in order. Where do you want the money to go?"

"I want the money to go to you kids," their father replied. "Remember that inheritance thing? I lied."

That is a true story. The kids received the inheritance, but it was their father's way of testing them. He wanted to make sure they grew up having the *deserve to win mentality.* Because the kids worked hard, they deserved their father's inheritance.

We may not get the exact outcome that we expected, but if we work hard, good things happen. If we are in a deserving place good things happen. Sometimes bad things happen -perhaps there are storms along the way, but if we stay in that deserving place and go after our goal, it makes a difference.

One great way to get into this mindset is to state your outcome clearly and what you are currently doing to achieve that outcome. Make a list of what you are currently doing to achieve the outcome, what more you could be doing, and what tools, resources, and people you are using to your advantage.

CHAPTER 10:

Be a Scorpion

There is a scorpion and a frog on a river bank and the scorpion looks over at the frog and says, "Mr. Frog, would you be kind enough to allow me to sit on your back and could you swim across the river so I can get on the other side?"

"No," the frog says, "because you are a scorpion and you are going to sting me."

The scorpion responds "that's true, but rest assured that I will not sting you because if I do, you will die and drown and I cannot swim and I will drown."

The frog thinks about it and says "you're right. I have to cross the river too. Hop on." So the Scorpion gets on his back and they begin their journey across the river. When they are about two thirds of the way across the river, all of a sudden the scorpion raises his tail and stings the frog. The frog looks up and says "why did you sting me? I'm going to die." The scorpion says "I couldn't help it! I'm a scorpion. I sting. It's just what I do."

This story packs a powerful message. Think about it, "I'm a scorpion. That's what I do." The scorpion had such clarity, he knew who he was and that stinging was ingrained in him. Knowing yourself takes a certain mindset.

You should ask yourself three questions. What is it that you do? What is your mission? What is your purpose? Once you figure that out, be a scorpion and be it to the point where there are no distractions. We as humans are hard wired a certain way so it's a great way to teach people to be so focused. So figure out what you want to do in life. When you have a clear goal, you can be a scorpion. When you have that clarity you cannot fight the urges or temptations to do anything else – because it's hard wired in you.

Another way of looking at this principle is comparing story identity with what we do. For example, a gambler gambles, but someone who gambles once in a while is not necessarily considered a gambler. An athlete works out, but someone who works out may not necessarily be an athlete. Alcoholics drink, but someone who drinks wine or beer occasionally may not be an alcoholic. There's a big difference between having an identity and just doing something every so often. Like the scorpion, his identity as a scorpion means that he stings. We see this time and time again with leaders. A leader leads, but someone who leads every so often may not be a leader. But once they make the shift in who they are as a leader, they buy into who they are and they can't help but do the things that those people in that identity do. These big shifts happen, especially as we start to get our careers set up and start to get the reference points of where we are. If we get the circle of excellence or the President's Award and keep getting it again and again we start to believe that this is who we are. We think to ourselves "I am a champion. I am a winner. I am a leader."

Early on, we may not have those reference points to lean on but over time the more points we build, the stronger our identity becomes and the more we step into the space of who we are. In the beginning stages of our careers, we don't have those reference points, so we borrow from someone else until we gain experience and build our own.

My children get frustrated with me sometimes because something will come up and I will automatically go into what they call the "teacher mode." That is, I start teaching a lesson from my own experience. I'm a teacher at heart, as are all the great leaders I know. That's what I do. I'm a scorpion. We are all scorpions. We just have to figure out what we want to be scorpions of.

PART 3:

Sound Decision Making (Effort)

CHAPTER 11:

Priority Management vs. Time Management

Our society teaches us that we have to be good time managers. There are libraries full of books and resources that are dedicated to proper time management. In all honesty, there is no such thing as time management. We have no control over time. Time continues with or without us. What we do have control over is how we prioritize our time.

I encourage you to strike the phrase "time management" from your vocabulary. Replace that phrase with "priority management." Focus on what your priorities are. When you know your priorities, you can focus on them. You fill your day with activities that are based around your priorities.

Stephen Covey, a well-known professor, author, and businessman, did an interesting demonstration. Covey began the demonstration by taking a jar and filling it with rocks. Then he asked the audience if the jar was full. The audience said that it was full; the rocks had filled the entire jar. Then Covey pulled out a bucket of pebbles and poured them into the jar. All of the pebbles fit into the spaces between the bigger rocks. Again, he asks if the jar is full. The audience catches on and says no, the jar is not full. Next, Covey brings out a bucket of sand and pours the sand into the jar. The sand fits into the cracks between the rocks and the pebbles. Once again, Covey asks if the jar is full, and the audience says no. The last thing Covey adds to the jar is a bucket of water. The water takes the shape of the jar and fills in all of the tiny cracks between the grains of sand.

Covey's demonstration is the perfect model of how to build your priorities. Your priorities are the big rocks. The only way the big rocks will fit into the jar is if you put them in first. If you put the water in, and then the sand and the pebbles, you will not be able to fit the big rocks in. Successful people know that the big rocks - their priorities always come first.

Successful people realize that they don't manage time. What they manage are their priorities. Think of it this way, you have been given 24 hours today. In those 24 hours, you have to take your priorities and focus on a critical few. Do not think in terms of time management. Instead, focus on your priorities every day.

Many people get caught up in the little things during the day - phone calls, emails, memos - and they don't get important tasks accomplished because they are distracted by those small things. Suddenly, the end of the day comes, and they wonder where the day went.

I have a simple rule to be productive and avoid getting distracted by the little things. I call it the "9AM Rule." Complete your most important task for the day by 9AM, and also do the most uncomfortable thing you have to do each day by 9AM. (Does it have to be 9AM? No. The actual time that you accomplish these two tasks will depend on your work schedule. If you begin work early, you may want to complete these tasks before 9AM, and you may complete them after 9AM if you begin working later.)

The most successful people live by this leadership lesson. They get their top priority done first thing in the morning. Then they get their most uncomfortable task out of the way. When you get that uncomfortable task out of the way, it's liberating. You feel calm, focused, and energized for the rest of the day. That uncomfortable task might be a difficult conversation with a coworker or a difficult phone call to a client. If you put off this uncomfortable task, you will be thinking about it all day, and consequently, you will accomplish fewer important tasks.

Your important or uncomfortable task might take place outside of the office. It could be your morning workout. So you motivate yourself to wake up early and get that workout done right away in the morning. That way, you feel more energized for the rest of your day. Additionally, you won't be sitting in your office all day thinking about how you're going to fit your workout into your schedule.

The first step to implementing the 9AM Rule into your daily life is training your mind. You have to work the rule into your mindset. But just thinking about it is not enough. You have to apply the rule. You have to motivate yourself, push yourself to do those two tasks first thing in the morning. This principle is all about acting on your intentions. Look at what you have to do, and then take action.

~~Time~~ Priority Management

CHAPTER 12:
Be Faithful to What is Helpful

Individuals that experience success, happiness, and fulfillment in their lives understand that it does not come free and easy, it takes sacrifice. What these people have discovered is that the result is more pleasurable than the effort. So they have learned to be faithful to the habits that they used in order to get their desired result.

A senior in college who is going to graduate with honors recognizes that the reason she is graduating with honors is because she has formed the habit of studying hard. For the past four years, she has taken time out of her day to study without disruption. She has formed that good habit. This student knows that when she studies, she gets the grades she wants.

The same goes for the star athlete. He performs well because he trains hard. He lifted weights at the gym, he studied film, and he ate right during the week. He knows that his good habits are rewarding because they give him the results he wants on the field.

In other words, good habits correlate with success. Be faithful to what is helpful - look at the systems, strategies, sacrifices, and habits that helped you achieve the results you wanted, and keep doing them.

Good habits and bad habits take time to form and are hard to break. Hard, but not impossible. Successful people have, quite simply, formed the habits of success. So, how can you break bad habits and replace them with good habits that will help you achieve your desired results?

Let's say there is a young financial advisor with the bad habit of waking up at 9AM every morning. He knows that if he were to wake up at seven, get in a workout, have a good breakfast, and make the four phone calls he needs to make, it would revolutionize his life. If he could just do this for three months, or six months, or a whole year, it would change everything for the better. He would be much closer to achieving his goals as financial advisor. How can this young man make the commitment to wake up at seven every morning? How can he begin to form that good habit and why is he struggling to break his old habit of sleeping in?

This young financial advisor probably has not found his *why* or his reason yet. He is not able to answer the question "why is this important to me?" Sure, he may have goals. Goals are nice because they are tangible, but goals can also be a hindrance because that is what people focus on. They put all of their energy into achieving one goal, which is only a small part of the big picture. Focus on a goal is short-term. After setting a goal, you must ask yourself why that goal is important. Why did you set that goal in the first place?

Let's say that the overall result you want to achieve is a 20% increase in business. What you have to ask yourself is why that increase is important to you. Why are you willing to make sacrifices to achieve that 20% increase? Perhaps you want to increase your business to 20% so your children can have opportunities that you did not have. That is a darn good reason to want to increase your revenue. So you have to focus on your *why*, because that is your motivation to make sacrifices. That is your motivation to be successful.

You have to train your mind to think about what you must have instead of merely what you want. Think about it. If you see something that you must have, you find a way to get it. You have just found your *why* and you go out and get it.

I have a very good friend who is a financial advisor. His *why* when he first went into business was very superficial, but it got him through the difficult first year of being a financial advisor.

He wanted to buy a brand new Chevy Camaro. He figured out that in his first year in the business, if he worked hard enough, he could make enough money to buy that Camaro. So he woke up early every day, stayed at the office late, made extra phone calls, and dealt with rejection, all because he could see himself behind the wheel of that car, and he did it. All of his hard work paid off and he was able to buy the Camaro. Now, 25 years later, he looks back and laughs. He says, "That was crazy! Now I would never endure that pain for a stupid car" but that doesn't matter. At the time, buying a Camaro was important enough to him to motivate him to make sacrifices.

We all have different reasons for working hard and making sacrifices. It does not matter what your specific *why* is. What matters is that you have one and you connect with it. Because when that connection is there, the results will follow.

CHAPTER 13:

When Values are Clear, Decisions are Easy

Roy Disney had a saying which helped guide him when it came time to make important decisions in one's life and that was, "when values are clear, decisions are easy." All of us in our lifetimes are going to have to make some important decisions. For that matter, there are about 25 decisions that you really have to get right in your lifetime. What those decisions are will vary for each person but the point behind that message is, those 25 decisions are the ones that are going to steer and shape your life and what you experience and the person you become. Some of those might be whether or not you decide to get married and have a family.

It might be where you live, the college you attend, all those types of things. And the point is, about every couple of years there comes a big decision that you have to make, and what you decide will really shape your life. Those are the ones that are going to require your utmost focus and attention. We have this tendency to occupy ourselves with lots of little decisions that paralyze us. So if you find yourself worrying about a decision you have to make, ask yourself, "Is this one of those 25 big decisions I have to get right?" Chances are probably not. So make the decision, move forward with it and learn from it. But if your answer to that question is yes, then you must ask yourself, "Am I making this decision based on my values? Am I getting the guidance and counsel from people I respect and admire?" That is the thought process that has to occur once you identify a really big decision in your life.

Before you can figure out if you are making a decision based on your values, you have to figure out what your values are as a person. Because once you identify what those values are, now ask yourself, "Is the decision I'm making in alignment with those values" and if the answer is no, then obviously you have a conflict. If the answer is yes, then the decision making process is actually pretty easy. It's not necessarily easy to follow through on your decision. When values are clear, decisions are easy.

Now, the action or sacrifice that your decision may require might be very, very difficult, but deep down you know that it is the right decision. One person who was good at difficult but necessary decision-making is Jack Welch. Welch talked about how when he was running General Electric, one of his values was making sure that no person was greater than the company. The company was really the sum of all its parts and people were those parts. Welch believed that great leaders have edge. He defined edge as the ability to fire one's own sister or brother if necessary if they weren't getting the job done. If you're running a major company and your sister or brother is in a key role but they're not being productive, you know you might put the company in harm's way if you don't remove them from that position. Again, when values are clear, decisions are easy. Firing your sibling is an easy decision to make, but a very difficult action to carry out. So, the most successful people in the world are individuals who understand what they stand for and what their values are, and in decision making time, always reflect upon those values to make sure the decision aligns with their values.

Motivational author and speaker Tony Robbins had 6 primary values that drive all of us. Robbins said that if you can figure out what your top 2 are, any decisions you make will be based on those top values. The 6 values are:

1. **Growth** – to know that you are expanding and that you are becoming all that you can be. You are growing.

2. **Contribution** – giving back to others.

3. **Connection** – building strong relationships with others.

4. **Variety** – things are always changing, but in a good way, so that nothing becomes mundane.

5. **Certainty** – things remain consistent in that you have a strong structure and process in place.

6. **Significance** – the knowledge that you are making a big difference, that your contributions are necessary and appreciated.

These are just some examples of core values. If you can decide what your very top values are, you will be prepared to make any big decision that comes your way.

CHAPTER 1:
The Little Things Done Right Allow the Big Things to Go Right

The devil is in the details. We've all heard that before and we hear it all the time because it's true. Details are your pathway to success. The details are not very glamorous or fun, but they are necessary. Getting the details right can prevent larger problems.

A perfect example of a person who focused on details is college basketball coach John Wooden. Many say Wooden was one of the greatest coaches that ever lived. Wooden won 11 National Championship titles at UCLA. On the first day of practice every year, Wooden began practice by teaching his players how to properly put on their basketball socks. Wooden did this because, if the players did not put their socks on correctly, their feet would blister while they were running up and down the court. If their feet blistered, they would get sore. If their feet were sore, the players would not be able to run as fast or jump as high or play at their best possible level. Wooden knew that if his players had sore feet, they would not play their best, and the team would suffer. That is why he always started each season by teaching his players how to put on their socks properly.

In the business world, and specifically in financial advising, concentrating on details is vital to success. The most successful financial advisors have critical numbers, which are what make each financial advisor's practice work. That critical number differs between financial advisors, of course, but what is important is that each financial advisor has a critical number, because they know that number is a true leading indicator. Making phone calls and taking notes and getting appointments are small things, but they are extremely important to reaching that critical number. Doing those small tasks may seem tedious, but you have to concentrate and do them well to reach your bigger goals.

CHAPTER 15:

The Common Denominator of Success: Pleasurable Methods vs. Pleasurable Results

This brings us to another principle: "The Common Denominator of Success." The Common Denominator of Success is this: Successful people have formed the habit of doing things that failures don't like to do. Nowhere does it say that successful people enjoy doing these things. I would even go so far as to say that successful people despise doing the things that failures don't do. Nevertheless, successful people understand the difference between pleasurable methods and pleasurable results.

Can you sit on the couch, drink a six-pack of beer, eat potato chips, and be in great physical shape? No, of course not. Can you take short cuts and not work very hard and have outstanding results - in school, business, relationships, or spiritual life? No. The world does not work that way. Short cuts are what I would categorize as pleasurable methods.

You have to determine what is more important to you. Is it instant gratification, or are you focused on pleasurable results, which oftentimes delay gratification?

For example, let's take a student that wants to graduate Magna Cum Laude. There is no easy way to do that. That is hard. It takes sacrifice. Working toward that goal means spending a lot of hours in the library studying. It means missing out on a lot of social events. There is no easy way to graduate Magna Cum Laude, but is graduating with honors a pleasurable result? It most certainly is. So the common denominator of success is focusing on pleasurable results and doing the things necessary to achieve those pleasurable results. People who focus on pleasurable results do not focus on methods. They realize that to achieve pleasurable results, they have to work harder and make more sacrifices.

This is something you learn through habit formation. This principle is about consistently doing something a little bit better, a little bit longer, a little bit more accurately, time after time after time. Over years, the results of this extra hard work are absolutely incredible. It is the financial advisor that prospects twenty minutes more every day. Twenty minutes. Maybe that is in the form of cutting short that conversation with a co-worker or waking up earlier in the morning or staying at the office a few minutes later at night. Those twenty minutes a day, over the course of a year, add up to many hours of prospecting which lead to more appointments made which, in turn, lead to more clients that advisor is serving.

The Common Denominator of Success does not come down to one moment or one thing that you do one time to solve everything. It is a habit of formation.

It seems like there are some people that make it look effortless. They're making the calls, writing the big cases, going to the gym, and it seems like they're enjoying the process. They're having fun in the moment even while they're working hard and making sacrifices to achieve great results. These people are a stark contrast to others who work nine-to-five jobs and seem miserable. They are achieving an outcome but they hate their lives. So how do we avoid being miserable? How do we get to the point where we enjoy the process?

I believe it occurs when we fully connect the head to the heart and it is captured in a quote that my mentor, Phil Richards shared with me. "The Master in the art of living makes little distinction between his work and his play, his labor and his leisure, his mind and his body, his education and his recreation, his love and his religion. He hardly knows which is which. He simply pursues his vision of excellence in whatever he does, leaving others to decide whether he is working or playing. To him, he is always doing both."

CHAPTER 16:

Total Effort Equals Total Victory

I often think about Vince Lombardi's famous speech, which is called "What it Takes to be Number One." At the end of the speech, Lombardi says that any man's finest hour, his greatest fulfillment to all he holds dear, is that moment when he has to work his heart out in a good cause and he's exhausted on the field of battle, but victorious. I think that's so true in describing when one's finest hour is.

Think about a time when you have set a goal and then gone and done everything you could to make that goal and you made it. That is one of the most remarkable feelings that a person can ever have.

Sometimes even if you don't necessarily "win," you still feel good because of all the effort you put in. For instance, say you set a goal and then poured everything you had into making that goal, but you didn't quite hit your goal. Did you lose? Not really, because you have put all of your time, energy, and effort into reaching your goal. The outcome is not always what matters. What does always matter is the effort you put into every task. Total effort equals total victory.

Unfortunately, sometimes there will be effort without results. You will never, however, get results without effort. It is all about habit formation. If you have a goal, do everything you can to reach that goal. Hopefully, even if you do not reach your goal, you will have formed some positive habits. That way, the next time you set a goal, you can work toward it with your better habits and you will be more likely to reach it.

Often times I see people who have ambitious goals. They really want to do something and they have great ideas, but they can't find the motivation. They don't apply the effort. How can those people find motivation? How can they put forth the effort to reach their goals?

First of all, if someone has a goal in mind but they can't find the motivation to pursue it, I think that he or she really does not want it. It's like saying I would like to have instead of I need to have. There is a big difference between a student that begins the semester by saying, "I am determined to get an A in this class" and the student who says, "It would be nice to get an A."

Many people think they have goals when they say, "I want this to happen." That's a wish, not a goal. A goal is wanting something, needing something so badly that you are willing to make sacrifices and work as hard as you possibly can to make that happen. It goes back to the chapter on pleasurable methods vs. pleasurable results. If a student is determined to get an A in her class, she recognizes that there will not be pleasurable methods of achieving that goal. She will have to spend two hours on homework every day. She will have to spend some nights and weekends in the library but that is okay because she will get the result she is aiming for.

If someone is struggling with motivation, the first thing I will say is, do you really want that pleasurable result? If they are unsure, then it probably is not very important to them. If they say, "Yes, that is important," then the next question is, why? Why is reaching that goal so important to you? The reason that student wants to get an A in her class is so that she can have a good GPA when she graduates. She gets it; she's connecting the dots. It's all about looking at the big picture.

The results may not come right way, but that's okay. If you work hard, good results will come. It's not if, it's when. It might take a week, a month, or even a year, but results will come if you form good habits and put forth the effort to reach your goals. If you keep working day in and day out, at some point success will be inevitable.

A while ago, my son wanted to buy a snowboard for the coming winter. He wanted it really badly, so I asked him what he could do to earn it. He offered to cut the grass. I asked about his grades and agreed to pay him for every 100% he got on a test. He earned enough to put the snowboard on layaway and three months later he paid it off. During those months he was saving up, he studied harder than he ever had and he always mowed the lawn on time. He put in the effort to achieve his goal.

CHAPTER 17:
25 Decisions

Remember from Chapter 13, there are 25 decisions that you have to get right in your lifetime. My mentor Phil Richards shared this with me years ago as he sensed I was agonizing over a decision and used it as a teaching point to not sweat the small stuff. This statement gives one clarity when needing to make a decision that chances are it is not a life changing decision so make a decision and move on. However there are times when a major decision must be made and the key is to know the difference and apply the right energy and resources. The key is to focus and be able to identify what those decisions are. This chapter is not just a list of 25 decisions that you will have to make in your lifetime, and are there exactly 25 decisions? Probably not. I often see people struggling with small decisions, such as what they are going to do over the weekend. I even see people get into arguments over petty things, and the question I always ask is, "Is this one of the 25 decisions you have to get right in your lifetime?" If not, then who cares? Why does it matter so much? The truth is, it doesn't.

The point is that you have to prioritize your decision making. Every few years, there is going to be a big decision that will influence the direction of your future. Those are the ones you really have to pay attention to.

Here are some examples of influential decisions: whether you want to go to college, if you want to get married, where you choose to live, whether or not you want to have children, your career choice, or accepting a promotion in a different location.

Once you make a big decision, you will begin going down a path. That path will lead to larger decisions. All too often, people get stressed about small decisions. In those situations, a good thing to ask yourself is if this is one of those 25 big decisions. Will it affect the course of your life? If the answer is no, then make a decision and move on. If the answer is yes, then take some time to think about it and ask others for their wisdom and advice.

Don't sweat the small stuff. Almost everyone has heard this saying. It's true. Consequently, it's important to be able to recognize the big stuff so you can give it the time and attention it needs.

Decision-making is like a muscle. You have to work it to keep it in shape. If you work it by making small decisions in a timely manner, you will feel better about making larger decisions.

CHAPTER 18:

Don't Let Your Short-Term Circumstances Dictate Your Long-Term Decisions

Let's say there is a young man whose long-term goal is to become a financial advisor. Unfortunately, his current circumstance is that he has just failed his Series 7 Exam. He should not let his short-term circumstance change his long-term goal. He has decided to become a financial advisor. His objective has not changed. So he has to ask himself what he must change to reach his goal. First, he has to re-take the exam and pass it.

Again, great real world example is Michael Jordan. His goal was to play college basketball and professional basketball, but in his tenth grade season, he got cut from the varsity team. Did he let that short-term circumstance dictate his long-term decision making? Of course not. He worked harder than he ever had before and he made the varsity team the following year. Before long, he was a high school McDonald's All American player.

Let's say a young woman wants to become a doctor, but she gets a C in organic chemistry. She needs to get a B or better to get into medical school. What she has to do is simple, retake the course. It may be a set-back, but it's not the end of the world.

Everyone learns to walk before they can even talk. We do it as babies. We pull ourselves up, usually by a table or wall at first, and then we take a few steps and fall. If everyone stopped trying to walk when they fell, we would all be crawling around instead of walking. Persistence is innate. Before we can even talk, we persist in our attempts at walking until we can do it without thinking. If we kept that attitude as we got older, we would never let minor set-backs dictate our long-term decision making.

I see it much too often where a young person lets a short-term circumstance dictate their long-term goal. The trick is to take yourself out of the moment and focus on your goal. You may have to make some more sacrifices or adjust a few things, but if you focus on your vision, you will achieve it. Keep your stamina up, persist, push on, and eventually you will find yourself where you want to be.

PART 4:

Sharp Skills

CHAPTER 19:

Fresh Fish for Sale - The Slow Erosion of the Fundamentals

Here is a story that captures the reason people don't achieve their goals and objectives. A gentleman owns a fish market on the waterfront. It is a simple fish market which is reflected by the sign that hangs over the market. The sign reads, "Fresh Fish for Sale." Over time, some of the patrons approach the owner of the market.

"You know," the patrons say to him, "we can tell that your market sells fresh fish. You're right on the waterfront and you go out every morning for the daily catch. You really don't need to have the word 'fresh' on your sign."

The market owner considers this and decides that his patrons are right. So he removes the word "fresh" from the sign. Now, the sign just reads "Fish for Sale." Time passes, and the same group of patrons approach the owner again.

"We know that your business is for profit," they explain. "We know you sell fish for profit. Do you really think you need the words 'for sale' on your sign?"

Again, the owner considers their insight and decides to remove the words "for sale" from his sign. Now the sign just says "Fish." More time passes, and the same group of patrons approaches the owner once again.

"Listen," they say, "It's obvious that you sell fish. We smell the aroma as we walk down the pier every day and we can see the fish as we approach your market, so we really don't think you need to advertise that you have fish." The owner ponders this and he decides to remove the word "Fish" and therefore he removes his sign altogether.

A year later, the market goes out of business.

The moral of the story is that people don't hit their goals because of the slow erosion of the fundamentals. This erosion does not happen overnight. It happens slowly over time. All of a sudden, a business owner realizes that he is ignoring the foundation of his business. He has neglected the most important aspects of his business, and over time, they have become rusty. So the point is that we all have to pay attention to the little things.

If a golfer breaks down the mechanics of her swing and examines how all of the little mechanics tied together create the fluid motion of her swing, she will hit the ball far down the middle of the fairway. Her attention to the details of her swing allows her full swing to be executed beautifully.

In a football game, there are many small parts that come together to make the game what it is. Two teams, over 100 players, and many individual plays. Each player has a role to play on each snap. If 1 player breaks down, it can cause the entire play to break down, which can be detrimental to that team.

If a businesswoman wants to have a fantastic quarter or a fantastic year, she has to design certain tactics to build her strategies to be successful with her clients. She has to spend a lot of time building these strategies in order for them to work. She has to make them perfect, or as close to perfection as she can get them.

In all of these scenarios, the little things need to come together to make a successful big picture. You have to be observant and pay close attention to details at all times. If you miss a detail here and there, those ignored details will start to add up. Over time, those ignored details will cause a slow erosion of the fundamentals, which will ultimately lead to failure. It all boils down to paying constant attention to details and fundamentals, and when you focus on the fundamentals; you must be brilliant on the basics. If you look at the most successful people in the world, you will quickly determine that what they do is not drastically different from others, but they are a little bit better at it. They are better with the basics and so they never allow that slow erosion of the fundamentals to happen. Successful people always stay grounded and emphasize the fundamentals.

CHAPTER 20:
4 Rules of Business

RULE 1: SAY PLEASE AND THANK YOU

This rule is all about customer service. The business has to understand that their customer service can make them stand out and be remembered. Too often today, we get excited about receiving reasonable customer service. It's exciting because we don't expect outstanding customer service anymore. When we go to customer service, we assume that things are going to take longer than they should, that things aren't going to be as good as we expect them to be, or that the people aren't going to be friendly. It is unfortunate that that has become the normative for business today.

But if you look at businesses that charge a premium for their products and services, you will see that one of the fundamentals that they apply is world-class customer service. They know how to say please and thank you. So take the rule of business and apply it to your personal life and professional life. Please and thank you is a great start, but these words mean more than just having good customer service.

RULE 2: BE FIVE MINUTES EARLY

In application, this rule is mostly figurative. For example, if you show up to a business meeting five minutes early, you have time to gather your materials and prepare yourself so that you are in the right frame of mind before the meeting starts. If you show up five minutes late, however, you are going to be worried about disrupting the meeting and the way others perceive you because you are late. It is going to take you at least 10 minutes to recover and get into the frame of mind for the meeting. If you had been 5 minutes early, you would have been completely prepared and calm for the meeting. Those 5 minutes early will aid your preparation in all situations.

RULE 3: FINISH WHAT YOU START

When someone asks you to do a task, the first thing you should ask yourself is "am I going to be able to see this task through completely?" If you cannot answer that question with a "yes," you should consider turning down that opportunity, because you need to be able to finish what you start. This is especially true of large projects.

So many people and so many businesses in this world don't think tasks through. Instead they get excited and get caught up in the appeal of the task. They don't think about the energy, devotion, time, and resources that task or initiative is going to take. They start down the road and when the initial enthusiasm wears off, they abandon the project and then the mission. That abandonment is what derails businesses and people.

The best businesses don't take on initiatives or projects that they know they can't finish. If they start a project, they finish it. It's that simple.

RULE 4: KEEP YOUR PROMISES

I always tell people, "be careful what you promise." Personally, I don't make promises very often unless I know I can absolutely deliver because that is my integrity and reputation. The Chinese have a saying, "lose your money and you have lost nothing, lose your health and you have lost something, lose your integrity and you have lost everything." Keeping your promises is all about integrity. When I do make promises, I keep them.

I've often heard the saying, "under promise, over deliver." I think there is a good lesson in that saying, which is to not promise very much and then provide more than you have promised, but I don't necessarily buy into that saying. I don't believe in downplaying things. I just believe in keeping my promises. A better saying is "Don't make promises you can't keep." If you make a promise, no matter how big or small, make sure you can follow through with it.

Businesses and individuals that apply these 4 rules of business in every opportunity they take on tend to do very, very well.

CHAPTER 21:

Learn a Lot About a Little and Do a Lot of It (Specialize)

I often say, "learn a lot about a little, and do a lot of it." This is also known as specializing. The most prosperous people today are specialists. They have a particular skill set that they have mastered. They are not trying to be all things to all people. They are not trying to serve all markets. They have learned as much as they can about a small slice of the world and they have practiced it endlessly.

Take medical specialists. They dedicate their entire lives to a particular specialty in medicine, and they go so deep into that area and they advance very far in the medical world by having a specialist mindset.

Specialization carries over into the business world as well. The most fruitful financial advisors are specialists. They learn as much as they can about a small part of financial advising and they focus on that for their entire careers. For instance, they might learn the ins and outs of a particular realm of financial advising - estate planning, retirement planning, succession planning, or even planning for business owners. Then, they do so much of that particular planning, usually with a particular group of people or to serve a specific market or product, that they become specialists.

Like so many things, specialization begins with a mindset. Decide what specific subject you want to learn a lot about, and then do that. Learn as much as you can and practice it as much as you can. Before you know it, you will be a specialist.

Some people know exactly what they want to do with their lives at a fairly young age. That is great for them, but most people are not like this. Lots of people have an idea of what they want to do, but they don't know specifics. There is nothing wrong with either type of person. The people who do not know exactly what they want to do have simply not yet found what they really love to do. They have not experienced something that excites them, or that makes them stop and think to themselves, I could be happy doing this forever. I could be happy doing this without getting paid.

If you have not yet found what you want to do with your life, don't worry. You will get there. I always say that the best way to figure out what you love to do is exposure. Exposure is simply experiencing a number of different things within a broad topic and then finding which one you like best.

Take a high school athlete who participates in four sports. He swims during the summer, plays football in the fall, does basketball in the winter, and plays baseball in the spring. Obviously, this is a young man who loves sports. He knows that much - he loves competition and team bonding and challenging himself physically. What he does not know quite yet is which sport he likes best. So throughout high school he participates in all four of these sports. As time goes on, he may recognize that he has an affinity toward one of these sports or that he simply likes one better than all the others. When he goes to college, he has narrowed his four sports down to one - he has decided to play baseball. He has learned a lot about baseball and he has put as much of his time as he can into practicing and playing only baseball. Because he experienced many different sports, he was able to figure out which one he liked best.

Another example is a beginning medical student. She is entering medical school with the plan of becoming a doctor. During her course of medical school she will decide whether she wants to become a radiologist, oncologist, pediatrician, or another specialty. She will make that decision based on her various classes and the types of medicine that she has been exposed to.

Deciding what you want to specialize in is all about looking at your interests and then getting exposure and seeing the different parts of those interests. Then, you can narrow your search for a career. From that point, you look at what you have an affinity towards, what aligns with your values, and what you really love to do.

In the business world, there are 3 Ps: Passion, Purpose, and Profit. Passion is what you're most excited about and Purpose is your natural ability. If you can find a job that connects both your Passion and your Purpose - something you're great at and also really excited about -you have really hit a home run. If you can make good money on top of that, you've hit a grand slam.

Earl Nightingale, one of the founding fathers of the motivational/self-help industry, stated years ago that to become an expert in anything one must dedicate 10,000 hours to that noble pursuit to obtain mastery level. In the past few years books by Malcolm Gladwell and other bestselling authors have reinforced and validated the time commitment one needs to reach expert/master status. This demonstrates that those that learn a lot about a little and do a lot of it (10,000 hours plus) will be viewed and sought out as the best of the best.

CHAPTER 22:

Set Up, Organize Up, Show up, Follow Up

This chapter is a breakdown of what has to occur for things to be accomplished. Think about a medical operation. If someone is going to have an operation, a number of things have to occur for that operation to happen. People have to take the time to make that surgery happen. Administrators need to pick a time, a date, and a hospital. The patient and clinic need to first work together to plan the surgery.

Next comes organization - the patient is going to be there at 10 o'clock, the operating room has to be prepared, the right doctor has to be there, the right staff needs to be there, the right equipment needs to be prepared and in the correct place. Next, people have to show up. The most important person that has to be there is the surgeon. The patient needs to be there, too, as well as the nurses and other supporting staff. Then, the surgery itself happens. After the operation is completed, there is the follow up. The patient goes into the recovery room for a period of time. Then, they take certain steps, do exercises, eat good foods, and follow the doctor's orders so that they can make a full recovery.

The question that needs to be answered before any of this can be accomplished is: who is going to do what? Who is going to complete each task? If you look at the most successful people in the world, you will discover that they all fall into one of these four categories.

The 1st category is the set up. Somebody has to set everything up. Whether it be a business meeting, teaching a class, participating in an athletic event, or performing surgery, it takes a lot of work behind the scenes to lead up to an event or experience to happen.

The 2nd category is organization. Again it takes a great deal of work mostly done behind the scenes to ensure the event and experience takes placed as planned.

The 3rd category is the show-up people. These are the specialists. The surgeon who shows up to the hospital before the surgery, prepares for the surgery, and then performs it. The financial advisor, who shows up for the meeting, guides and educates his client. The athlete who steps foot in the arena, and then competes. These are the "performers" and without them the event or experience does not take place. These are the ones that the entire operation is built around and rightfully so. They are also the ones that usually get paid the most and the ones that are in the spotlight.

The 4th and final category is the follow up. Once the event or experience ends, a host of activities need to occur to wind down the event and to begin making and preparing the next steps for future opportunities.

When Frank Sinatra was performing, his job was to sing because he was the performer. Frank wasn't selling tickets. He wasn't moving the piano into the orchestra hall. He wasn't showing people to their seats. There was an entire crew of people doing that for him. They all had assigned jobs in one of the previous 4 categories. All of these people working together -including Frank Sinatra - made his shows successful.

The most successful people build models by recognizing that their job is to show up and to repeat that job over and over again. Next, they recognize that they need to build an environment and an infrastructure and organize the people around them to make sure that they are always in a place where they can succeed.

A pilot's job is to fly the plane. You're not going to see a pilot checking in luggage because that's not a good use of his or her time. You're not going to see a surgeon scrubbing down the operating room after an operation. That's not a good use of his or her time. You're not going to see Frank Sinatra breaking down the orchestra hall and loading the equipment into the truck to haul to the next concert. You're not going to see a financial advisor spend 20 minutes going through forms with a client after the meeting. You're not going to see a dentist taking x-rays. For all of these examples, all 4 steps need to be done - people from all 4 categories need to do their jobs.

Prosperous people know what their job is. They show up and do their job and only their job. They focus on their specialties. That ties back to what we covered a few chapters ago -learning a lot about a little and doing a lot of it. In short, devote 10 hours a day to your profession and do things that align with your skill set or passion.

Let's say you want to start a business. At first, you are going to have to do a lot of things yourself, but in order for your business to grow and become fruitful, you will have to hire enough people and divide the work up among your employees. Then, you will be able to give your employees smaller tasks so that you can concentrate on larger tasks that will help get the business off the ground. You have to learn what activities generate the highest revenue, and then focus on those activities. You have to divest your business, divest your opportunities, and pay people to do it. This is a leap of faith, of course, but once you do it, you feel liberated because you have more time to do things that will generate more revenue and grow the business.

When it comes to hiring help, sooner is better. In my world, I encounter so many advisors who struggle with hiring a support person. They need the help because they spend too much time filling out paperwork when they could be prospecting, acquiring new clients, or meeting with new clients. However, they don't want to pay someone $15 an hour. After some guidance and encouragement from me, they finally hire that full-time support person. A year later, these advisors typically say, "I wish I hadn't waited as long as I did. What a priceless investment."

It is all about leaps of faith. There are times when you just have to take a leap of faith if you really believe in yourself and what you want to accomplish. You need to prioritize your time.

In our firm, we have financial advisors who are 6 months into their career and they are hiring staff. They might go out and hire an intern for 10 hours a week. They make the investment to pay that intern $10 an hour. So that's $100 a week and $400 a month that this advisor pays their intern, but they have created an extra week for themselves because they have freed up 40 hours. If you have 40 extra hours to be productive in your revenue generating activities, I think the return of $400 is going to be a lot better when you get your money back. That is 40 extra hours of introducing your services to new people.

CHAPTER 23:
Have Daily Critical Numbers

You should have daily critical numbers that make your business or life work. For example, in the financial advising world, advisors set goals that are either a certain amount of revenue they want their practice to generate for the year or the number of clients they want to reach. Reverse engineer it so you know that each week you have a certain goal you have to hit. (You can even break it down into a daily goal – say 8 first appointments per week, so each day you need to have 2 first appointments to reach your goal). At the end of each day you can ask a very simple question – did I win today or did I lose today? Know that some days you will win some days you will lose, but what happens is that when you win you feel good and know you did something worthwhile and you build on that momentum. If you lose, it's not the end of the world, but it creates a sense of urgency. You realize that you need to focus a little more, first thing tomorrow morning I need to go through my client files and ask for recommendations / referrals / introductions. Losing for the day brings an awareness that you are off track a little.

Most people slowly begin to go off track because they are not paying attention to a daily critical number. If you pay attention to a daily critical number, you will notice that you are off track when it is early enough to get back on track without much sacrifice or extra effort. The people who do not pay attention to daily critical numbers notice that they are off track maybe a month after they have gone off track. At that point, it is a lot more challenging to get back on track and it takes much more work and sacrifice.

This is a lot like making sure you are going to the doctor for annual checkups. Let's say there is something wrong with your health - the doctors detect cancer. If they detect it early enough, survival rates are very good, but if it goes undetected for a long time the survival rate goes down dramatically.

Let's take a student. She knows she needs to get her grade point average up to 3.5 and her critical number to do that is to invest in 2 hours of study per day. If at the end of the day she realizes that she did not study for 2 hours, she knows she needs to ramp it up. Having a daily or weekly critical number in your professional and personal life will force you to ask the question, "did I win today or did I lose today?" Just by doing that it allows you to build momentum on your victories. In your losses and in your defeats, it'll force you to make adjustments much sooner so little problems don't become big problems.

You don't want to over complicate things, so in your business world you need to find 1 or 2 key metrics that really make your business work. Keep it simple and then whenever you have a goal, reverse engineer it so you know what your daily critical number is.

For example, someone's personal goal might be to run a marathon. So he may have a running schedule in front of him at all times so that when he wakes up in the morning he knows how many miles he needs to run that day in order to get the mileage he needs for the week to stay on pace to cross the finish line in the time that he desires. Let's say the daily running schedule is to run 6 miles. So if he runs 6 miles today, good for him. If he doesn't, he will know that he will have to run more tomorrow to get back on track. Those daily running schedules allow the runner to do what is necessary each day to build the foundation and then build upon it to have a successful race, which is a great strategy to apply with anything in life. Don't over complicate it because if you do then you will be running around in a lot of different directions.

Many people ask how to keep from getting lost. The key is

to focus on a critical few numbers. There are multiple things being thrown at us in our world and if you have the ability to focus on the critical few it will allow you to prioritize properly. It's all about priority management, which we talked about earlier. If you can manage your priorities, you can hit those goals and objectives that you want to accomplish.

CHAPTER 24:
What is Measured Improves

Once something is measured, it is improved, and if you measure it you can manage it. If you have a goal and it is important to you, you have to measure it. Going back to examples we used earlier, maybe your goal is meeting a certain grade point average. The way to measure that is tracking, going online and checking your grades consistently, talking to your professors, and studying 2hours per night – that critical number you established. You are going to have all your key metrics in front of you to make sure you are on the right track and making progress.

What I see a lot of times is someone who has a goal or objective that they want to accomplish, but there is no real way to measure it. If you can't really measure whether you are making progress or not, that puts you in a tight spot, but if you measure something it immediately brings attention and awareness to the matter. So someone running a business might have an objective to hit a revenue goal. If they're measuring their revenue on a daily basis, they can simply ask and answer the question "what did the factory or business generate today?" I see it all the time with business as well as personally with individuals where they are not measuring their goal, but if they begin to measure it, it will start improving because of the heightened awareness of the matter. In short, what gets measured gets improved. It works with anything and I would go so far as to say that if you're not willing to measure it, then don't do it because it's a waste of time.

Think about weight lifting, if we didn't have the numbers on the plates, if there weren't a 45, 35, 10 or 5, it would just be dead weight - it would make no difference. There is a reason why we always say how many reps and sets we do and how long we've been going to the gym.

Let's say your goal is to bench 300 pounds and your max starts out at 225 pounds. You know that you have to increase by 75 pounds to reach your goal. Every lifting session you do you write down the weight you did and the number of sets and reps to measure your progress. Then you add a little more weight each time you lift weights, and over a certain amount of time you will start to see progress, but if you weren't writing things down and measuring you wouldn't know if you were making any progress. Measuring progress motivates and inspires you and helps you build on your momentum. Many things in the world are set up by measurements, and that is why they are an important component.

CHAPTER 25:
3 Rules of Sales Success

RULE 1: ALWAYS BE SOLVING A PROBLEM

If you are not solving a problem, it is going to be extremely hard to sell your product or your service. Organizations have to write out what the problem is that they are solving. The next question is, does the client or customer acknowledge that you are solving a problem? Do they see that they have a problem and that you can solve it? Sometimes, you will be talking to an individual and trying to sell goods or services and they will just be in denial in that they will feel that they do not have a problem that you can solve. So you can talk and talk and demonstrate and illustrate and present but you just have to learn to move on from those situations.

RULE 2: MAKE SURE THE CLIENT/CUSTOMER ACKNOWLEDGES THEY HAVE A PROBLEM THAT YOU CAN SOLVE

The main way to do this is to target customers that will most likely acknowledge that they have a problem that your goods or services can fix. Be very clear with what problem you are solving.

Often in sales we recognize that a problem does exist and our product or service solves the problem. However just because we see the problem doesn't mean the prospective client will see the problem or issue. It is up to us to do our best to educate, motivate and inspire the prospect to take action on the problem but sometimes people are in denial. The goal and point here is to not waste too much time on those that most likely will never come out of a state of denial.

I see far too many talented people spending an inordinate amount of time trying to convince someone of their problem to no avail. One needs to have an abundance mentality and recognize that there are plenty of people in this world that can benefit from their products and services. The prospect will acknowledge this and actually appreciate the products, services and relationship being provided.

Life becomes so much more enjoyable when they do business with those they truly appreciate. Life is too short working with those that do not appreciate or respect the value you bring. In these cases learn to say "next" and walk away. Even if the person becomes a client it will be short term or high maintenance.

RULE 3: MAKE SURE THE CLIENT HAS THE FINANCIAL MEANS TO PAY FOR THE SOLUTION TO THEIR PROBLEM

A customer might acknowledge a problem only to find out they do not have the financial means to move forward or work with your business to solve that problem. That goes along with targeting as well. You have to target an audience that will be able to pay for your goods or services.

An example of connecting all three of these rules would be a luxury automobile dealership. Are they solving a problem? Sure, they are solving someone's transportation needs and the customer understands that, but the issue is the affordability factor. Now they are going to target market that luxury automobile dealership into zip codes and areas. They know the average household income or net worth is a certain amount and they know that their customers have the means to buy their cars. So they place their dealership in a wealthier or higher net worth area because they know the people there will be able to afford luxury automobiles. Often times, businesses don't realize the importance of connecting all 3 of these rules.

It all depends on the right product for the right person. You no doubt have to be aware of that. It is such a simple concept but so true – you must keep those 3 components in place to make sure that you are on the right track.

PART 5:

Leading with Vision and Humility

CHAPTER 26:
Be the Chief Evangelist Officer

The most successful people in the world - whatever their mission may be - they are the **Chief Evangelist Officer** (CEO). This is not the Chief Executive Officer, though they may hold that title. I myself hold the title of CEO, but I do not view my job as being the Chief Executive Officer. First and foremost, I view my job as being the Chief Evangelist Officer. When you're a leader and leading a specific cause, vision, or mission, you have to know what you stand for. You have to know what your values are, and you have to constantly be evangelizing those values, culture and that vision.

Some of the most brilliant business professionals in the world - like Steve Jobs, Bill Gates, and Warren Buffet are the Chief Evangelist Officers. That is their primary focus. You can see this in some of the world's greatest leaders, Gandhi, Martin Luther King, Jr., Jesus Christ, and the Dalai Lama. You see it in head coaches and presidents of universities. The number one priority is focusing on the organization's main goal.

CEO also stands for **Chief Enthusiasm Officer**. You have to have enthusiasm to continue working on your cause. You have to be excited about what you're doing. You have to be passionate, and you have to be able to convey that passion to your employees or coworkers and your enthusiasm should be contagious.

CEO also stands for **Chief Executive Optimist**. Again, you have to be excited about what you're doing. You also have to believe in what you're doing. You have to be optimistic that you're going to achieve your goals and the results you're striving for.

CEO also stands for **Chief Energizing Officer**. You have to be energetic about your cause. More importantly, you have to be able to energize the people around you and make them excited about the cause.

CEO also stands for **Chief Empowering Officer**. You have to work to empower others. Help the people around you accomplish their goals and objectives. Give them responsibilities and latitude to achieve their goals.

CEO also stands for **Cultural Executive Officer**. Leadership is not only about building a culture, but about keeping a culture. Building is one thing, but after that you have to make decisions that can affect the culture. That's when you need a core set of values to base your decisions upon so that you can maintain what you have established.

CEO can stand for a number of things, but it all starts with evangelizing; the executive stuff is secondary.

The actual CEO of a company definitely needs to play all of these roles, but what about other people in the company? Can someone who is just starting out in their career be a different kind of CEO? Yes, they have to be. Everyone has to be the CEO of Me, Inc. Everybody has to have that mindset. You have to think of it this way, you are a business. You have honed your skill set to this particular organization. They are paying me to do this, but this organization is my customer. You only have one customer because only one person is paying you, but you're running your own business.

For example, if you are an IT technician for a company, you have to think of your job this way: I have my own IT Company, and I just happen to be hired by my one client, ABC, Inc. Therefore, I have to provide the best service possible, because if not, ABC, Inc. may decide that they don't need my services anymore.

If you're a business owner and you lose 1 client, it's not a big deal as long as you have done a good job of diversifying and you have 100 clients. If you only have 1 client and you lose that client, that's a big deal. You've just lost your revenue. So I think that it's even more important for people who do not have the title of CEO, adopt the mindset of being a Chief Evangelist Officer.

We are all Chief Evangelist Officers no matter where we are in our careers or where we are in life. It's just about specializing and realizing our passions. That's where it starts. It's easy to be an evangelist when you're excited about something. What if someone isn't excited? What if it's their first job out of school and they're working at a fast food restaurant or waiting tables? What if they've been at a job for ten years and they can't evangelize because they just don't like it? What do those people do?

Those individuals need to realize that the role they are currently in is only a means to an end. I had jobs throughout high school and college to get myself through school. I mowed lawns, I painted houses, and I waited tables. Of course, those jobs were not my lifelong passion, but I was passionate about getting my degree and going into my desired field, and those jobs helped me pay for that. Remember that those jobs are a stepping stone. What keeps you energized is knowing that there is a light at the end of the tunnel. Throughout college, I knew that I did not have to mow lawns or paint houses or wait tables for the rest of my life because that was not my passion. Short term, I had to stay focused and do a great job for the people I was serving, because that's what winners do. That's what successful people do. No job is irrelevant. Whatever you do, do it with excellence.

You wake up, and even though you may not be super excited about the job you're going to today, you have to remember that it's just a means to an end. You have to do the very best you can, because otherwise you might start heading down a slippery slope. If you start forming bad habits in your part time job that you aren't excited about, those bad habits will carry over to other things. So do the best you can in every job. You pick up that paint brush and paint the wall and make it look fantastic, even though two years from now you will never want to even see a paint brush again.

You can choose to be an evangelist for anyone you interact with, because you don't know where you can end up if you act as an evangelist. People gravitate toward that. Imagine that someone walks up to you and says, "Wow, it looks like you're working really hard flipping those burgers. Why do you work so hard?" You can tell them that the reason you work so hard flipping burgers is not because you love doing it, but because you're paying your way through law school and you envision yourself as a world-class trial attorney one day. That defines you. People observe those good habits, and your mindset carries through in everything that you do.

CHAPTER 27:
Be a Mentored Mentor

If you look at the most successful individuals in the world, you will find that, in almost every case, they have been mentored. All of them acknowledge that they've had a mentor. They have had people that have climbed to the top of the mountain before them, so to speak, and have acted as guides. These people that have become successful in their own right acknowledge that they did not do it alone.

Sir Edmund Hillary was given credit for being the first person to climb Mount Everest. What many people don't know is that Sir Edmund had a guide named Tenzing Norgay. Norgay led Sir Edmund Hillary up the mountain and took care of him. Norgay was his mentor and led Hillary in a true servant-leadership fashion.

Successful people hear the call to help other people, but they know they first have to be mentored themselves. They have to learn about their trade from an expert before they can begin to teach and help others.

You are never too old to have a mentor. No matter what stage you are in your life, you always want to have people around you that have climbed the next mountain, made it to where you want to go, have more knowledge, more wisdom, and outstanding results. You want to pick out those people and ask them for guidance. Ask them to serve as your mentor.

In addition to having mentors, truly prosperous people are mentors themselves. They give back. Their mindset is "other-focused." The perfect position to be in is one where you are being mentored and are mentoring others at the same time. When you are mentoring others, it requires you to stay sharp and focused. It requires you to be a role model.

When it comes to mentoring, there are an additional 3 Ps: passion, pain, and priorities. These are the keys to good mentoring. Ask yourself, what is this person's Passion? What do they want to accomplish? What is their why? Once you know that, you can help them pursue their passion and reach their goals.

The next P is Pain. The next thing a mentor needs to know about the person they're mentoring is, what is their pain? What are their challenges? What are their short-comings? What are their concerns? Once you know those, you can help them work through those challenges and concerns. You can advise them on how to keep moving forward.

The final P is Priorities. What are their priorities? What do they want to put first? What do they need to put first? Knowing these will give structure to your guidance.

If you can understand their passion, pain, and priorities, you will be a very effective mentor. This in turn will help the individual achieve the goals they are pursuing, which is very rewarding and fulfilling for you as their mentor. You want to help the person you're mentoring get to the top of their mountain.

When it comes to obtaining a mentor or becoming a mentor, there is no magic way to go about it. It is kind of like asking for referrals; it's just asking in whatever way is most comfortable for you. When you see someone you want to emulate and that you feel you can learn from, you have to work up the courage to ask them if they've considered being a mentor.

One word of caution, if you are asking someone to serve as a mentor to you, be ready to play the game and commit. If the person accepts your offer and says, "Yes, I'll mentor you, here are my expectations of you..." you have to be ready for those expectations. It's a 2-way street. You can't ask someone to be your mentor and then tell them it's only on your terms. You can't just be in it for yourself. You have to be ready to play the game.

Likewise, if you would like to mentor someone that you feel has a lot of potential, and you would like to help them reach that potential, there is nothing wrong with reaching out to that person. Ask them about their goals, their passions, their pain, and their priorities. Get to know them. See if there is a connection. Say that you are open to working with this person and that you are willing to be their mentor. There is no right way to ask the question. You just have to be courageous and do it.

Now, once someone agrees to be mentored or someone agrees to mentor somebody, it's important to have a conversation about expectations. How is the mentored relationship going to work? Will it be formal or informal? How often will you meet, and where? Meetings might involve getting together once a month for lunch, or a drink, or coffee, meeting up at the office before work on Monday to talk about the upcoming week, or meeting on Friday afternoon to talk about the past week. It's really up to the 2 of you. I would say that the best thing to do at your meetings is sharing victories and defeats with each other, but the first and most important discussion you need to have is about expectations. That way, both of you are on the same page in terms of what you expect from the other person, and what the other person expects from you.

So, how do you pick the right mentor? Is it someone that has climbed your Mount Everest? Is it someone that is winning the game at a certain level? What qualities should you look for in a mentor?

The main thing to look for is a person that you want to emulate in some aspect of your life, and you may have mentors in different areas. You may have a professional mentor at work. You may have a spiritual mentor because you want to emulate the way that person leads their spiritual life. You might have a mentor in the physical fitness realm, where your mentor makes sure you stay healthy and fit. You might have a mentor who you really admire in terms of how they handle their family and personal relationships. So you can have different mentors for different areas of your life. What you will find is that the best mentors do a good job in all of those areas. Somebody could be a great mentor in business but have challenges in their personal life, but chances are, those problems are going to carry over into their business, so that person may not be the best mentor.

Your mentor is your role model. When you find yourself in a difficult situation, you want to ask yourself what your mentor would do in that situation. If you really respect and admire your mentor, you will want to emulate them and their problem-solving skills.

In an earlier chapter, I stressed the importance of asking and answering these two questions, who are you becoming and who are you being? Are you becoming the person you want to be down the road? Are you working toward your goals? The decisions that you make today all focus on the question "Who are you being?" Are you being the person that makes decisions to help you become the person you want to be in the future? Both of these questions help you stay on track.

CHAPTER 28:

Lead First - Friend Second - Earn Respect First

The incredible basketball coach, Bobby Knight, coached for decades and he worked with various generations of student athletes. He was asked what his observations were of working with so many different generations of student athletes. Knight responded, "I noticed that today, kids are growing up in a world where too many of their parents are trying to be their friends, and when the parent tries to become the kid's friend, they end up having to be the kid's parent for the rest of the kid's adult life." Consequently, if you're a parent to your child first, you will have the joy of being their friend for their adult life.

All leadership roles are like that. It is important to be a leader first, especially early on in the formative years. If you do your job of being a leader first, your people respect that. They admire and appreciate it. Later on, they understand why you did the things you did, and why you held them accountable and had such high expectations for them. It's not fun to do those things, but you push people to do those things as a leader. That is good leadership, and it pays off for you and for them. Later on, your people will realize that you are someone they can trust because you care about them. Once they realize that, you have the joy of being friends with your people. But if you try to become friends first, you will never be able to be their leader.

The first challenge of this principle is the popularity factor. This is especially true for younger people going into the workplace who are young developing leaders. Some of them are going to be asked to be leaders amongst their peers and people who are older and more experienced than they are. Being captain of an athletic team is a great example of this. That's a tough spot. I have a lot of respect for today's youth who are captains of teams. During the day, they're best friends at lunch and hanging out after school, but on the field, they have to be a leader among their peers. The coach might tell the captain to talk to a teammate about their attitude or effort. The challenge is figuring out how to be an authoritative leader without ruining your relationships.

Would you rather be respected or liked? Leadership is about respect first, and respect is not based on title, it is earned. Sometimes certain titles warrant respect, but let's face it - people respect individuals because they have earned it. You earn that respect by being firm, having high expectations, and being a leader first. Once you earn that respect, friendship will form because you are trustworthy. Your people know that you they can confide in you; they know that you are not going to hold back or blow smoke. They know that if there is an issue, they can tell you about it. That is good leadership.

You have to ask yourself if there are instances where you're being too much of a friend and not enough of a leader. For me, there are instances in my life where I'm not being a leader and I'm being too much of a friend, and it impacts the people I'm trying to lead. It doesn't impact me all that much, but it impacts them. I need to remember to step up and be the leader first because that's my job. Someone has to do it. Someone has to be the one to tell my kids how to behave. If I'm leading a group of people and one of them reports to me and he's not performing, and I don't tell him that because I don't want to be the bearer of bad news, then shame on me. I'm not doing my job.

When your commitment is "other" focused, meaning it's about them, you can be a great leader. You know it's not about you and you try to convey that, and you hope, deep down, your people respect that. It's like telling your friend that you think he has a chemical dependency. It takes courage to sit that friend down and tell him that you think he needs help because you've noticed his behavior and decision-making lately, and it's not good. But if you do sit down with your friend and tell him these things, it demonstrates that you care deeply about him. That is the most sincere type of friendship. When someone who really cares tells you the truth and risks damaging the friendship, it is infinitely better than the group of friends who don't want to say anything about your friend's chemical dependency because they might hurt his feelings. Later on, your friend will thank you, because you were a great friend. You were courageous. You were a leader.

Remember, it's always about them. I keep repeating that because it's vital to being a successful leader. Even if the person you led never comes to respect you, you will know that you did your best as a leader because you were always focused on that person's well-being.

Leaders do not conform. Conformity makes leaders ordinary. The first person who tried to climb Mount Everest did not stop and say, "Well, that looks really hard. Besides, no one has ever done that before." Instead, that person looked up and said, "I think I can do it."

CHAPTER 29:
Are You a Thermostat or a Thermometer?

In a leadership position, you have to realize that you are the one who sets the pace. You set the temperature for the organization, the team, the association. Depending on whether you're a thermostat or a thermometer determines how you set the overall tone for your organization.

A thermometer measures temperature. A thermostat, on the other hand, sets the temperature for the room. Generally, you do not want to be a thermometer.

If you are leading an organization and you do not like the outcome, direction, or results you're getting, you need to ask yourself if you are a thermostat or a thermometer. Are you merely reflecting what is going on or are you establishing a culture and expectations?

As leaders, our responsibility is to set the expectations. We have to be the thermostat. The underlying principle of this idea is the Law of limited performance. This law states that one will rise to the level of expectations set forth by one's leader. So oftentimes, leadership consists of creating a positive culture and setting high expectations.

This brings us to another principle: A leader is a culture builder and a culture keeper. The leader's job is to build the culture by setting the temperature and not just reflecting what others are doing. Once you have built that culture, your job as a leader is to keep that culture going strong. Keeping the culture becomes more challenging later on. I would even argue that it's easier to build the culture than to keep it. Keeping the culture is about holding your organization accountable. The only way you can keep a culture is by having values and basing your decisions off those values. When values are clear, decisions are easy.

One main challenge that people face when trying to be a thermostat is popularity. This goes back to what we covered in the last chapter, be a leader first and a friend second. A lot of people hesitate to make a decision that would move their organization forward because they are worried about not being liked. So you cannot let popularity hold you back. You have to be other-focused all the time.

There are numerous situations where a leader can change the temperature of the room by being a thermostat instead of a thermometer and it has positively impacted the group and the leader's self-awareness. I see it all the time. A leader will simply pull out the best in others by creating a higher expectation. Everyone needs someone in their life to expect greatness from them, and the more people they have in their life that can play that part, the better off that person is going to be.

The problem in our society is that all too often we pass off the responsibility of expecting greatness. For example, parents might think that teachers and the school system should play that role, and teachers might think the parents should play that role, or coaches think parents should play that role and parents think coaches should play that role. Somebody has to set high expectations for the people that are developing in the world. The fact is, we have to take that responsibility upon ourselves.

For example, in the business world, if there is a new advisor that wants to start out doing 5 first-appointments per week, her leader should encourage her to bump that goal up to 6 or 7 first-appointments per week. That way, the new advisor will get her career off to a fast start. The advisor is new, so she doesn't know any better. Her leader needs to hold her to a higher expectation so that she succeeds.

Successful leaders are leaders who challenge the status quo and raise the bar. Good leaders don't sit back and create barriers by saying, "well, that's never been done before." Good leaders say, "Let's try that."

True leadership can change the room. It might not be instantaneous, but if a leader is doing his job right, his group will be able to see the culture shift to the betterment of everyone in the room.

Leadership, in essence, is helping others become the best version of themselves. All leaders lead to a vision or to a journey. The individual or group has a journey, and the leader guides them toward their goal. If someone says about you, "That person helped me become a better person," then you have excelled as a leader.

As with all things in life, there may be roadblocks in your journey as a leader. If you feel like you are not making progress as a leader, the first thing you should ask yourself is, "am I getting the results I am striving for?" If the answer is no, then you have to ask more questions. Am I being the thermostat? Did I set the pace? Did I create the environment? Am I creating the metrics? Am I measuring the right things?

It's all about looking in the mirror and recognizing the leadership within. You are the influencer; you are the thermostat. You are in control. You have the power to be proactive instead of being reactive. Because being a thermometer - merely reflecting what's going on - is not leadership.

I often give motivational presentations to groups of college students and young people just beginning their careers. Right before I go on stage, I ask myself, why am I here? If I'm presenting to a group, what is the reason for this presentation? I am here to educate them on this particular topic, to provide information, to help them, to make them better. Asking "Why am I here" is the foundation for 'other' focus. It's not about me; it's about them. It's always about them. Why am I here today? To focus on you, to help you get better, to help you reach your objectives. In asking myself "why am I here?" I am able to find that focus for the betterment of the individual or group that I'm spending time with. That question is what will get you into the thermostat mindset because then you can help lead, influence, and control how things go.

Raise the expectations for yourself and the people around you and you will become an outstanding leader.

CHAPTER 30:

The Law of Limited Performance

As a leader, what expectations are you putting forth? Everybody is going to rise to the level of expectation set forth by their leader. If on the first day of practice, a cross country coach tells his runners that they're going to run 5 miles, that's how far the runners will go. If that coach says that they're only going to run 2 ½ miles, that's how far the runners will go. If there is a low level of expectation, there will be a low level of performance. If, however, the leader holds her organization to high expectations, they will give her good results.

Do not impose your personal limitations on others. Just because you think you can't accomplish something doesn't mean that you can't help someone else accomplish the same thing. Great leaders recognize this. Going back to the thermostat versus thermometer—great leaders recognize that they have to be the thermostat and set the expectations at a high level, because people will rise to whatever level of greatness they are surrounded by.

A big challenge in leadership is balancing big aspirations with reality. For example, a mother taking her four year old son to swimming lessons for the first time and saying that he is going to win Olympic gold. It's great to have such high aspirations, but her son has to take a lot of steps first. Most importantly, he has to learn how to keep from drowning.

The main challenge is not being realistic with goal setting, but determining what goals to set. You have 3 goals. The 1st goal is the objective, or the minimum accepted level. A student might set his objective at a 3.0 minimum GPA. That is his minimal accepted standard. If he does not reach that, there will be serious consequences. If he does not reach his minimum GPA, he will most likely reevaluate what he is doing. The 2nd goal is called the goal. The student's goal is a 3.5 GPA. The 3rd goal to set is called the BHAG, or Big Hairy Audacious Goal. For the student, the BHAG is to graduate with honors with a 3.8 GPA. So he has 3 goals he's shooting at – 1st, the minimum, the objective, 3.0 GPA. If he doesn't reach that, he has to stop and wonder why he is even in this field of study, or why he's in college at all. Next, his goal is a 3.5 GPA. Finally, there is the BHAG of a 3.8 GPA that he can make if, on top of his hard work, all the moons are aligned and things go well.

The objective should be something that's not necessarily easy to accomplish, but something that is very realistic. The goal should require more effort. It should be realistic and challenging. The BHAG should be a stretch - it should be difficult but not impossible to accomplish. Setting these 3 different goals gets you into the right frame of mind and keeps you on track. Additionally, they keep you from setting a goal so unrealistic that right away you get frustrated and abandon the goal altogether.

Let's go back to building and keeping a culture. This is easier said than done. Often, I see leaders focus on one of these more than the other, and it causes problems. They do well in maintaining the culture, but it's not exactly the culture they want. Or they are building a culture but they don't necessarily have the accountability systems or the decision-making to maintain that culture, so the culture is short-lived. As I stated before, building a culture is set around vision; keeping a culture is set around values.

The challenge that many leaders run into is not really taking the time to figure out a clear vision and list of objectives. It's about finding your why and your Big Trophy Day. Why are you getting up in the morning? Why are you willing to make sacrifices? Your goal is your Big Trophy Day. It's what you want to accomplish. That is your vision.

The other challenge for keeping a culture is identifying what your core values are. If you don't identify your core values, you will not be able to maintain the culture. Keeping the culture is based on decision-making, so you need to have a set of values to guide your decision-making.

For example, a student wants to graduate with honors. One of his core values is education. His vision is to graduate in four years with honors. His value is clear, so his decisions are easy to make. Let's say it's Friday night and there's a big party going on, but he has a paper to write for Monday. He has to work on Saturday and Sunday, so that will take up a lot of his time. So his choices are to go to the party and hang out or stay home and spend time working on his paper so he can maintain a high GPA. The decision is easy. So when values are clear, decisions are easy.

Doing it is hard. The decision is easy, but following through requires discipline and sacrifice. So first, identify your vision so you can build on it. Second, identify your core values so you can make decisions based on them.

CHAPTER 31:

Goethe's Creed

"If I accept you for who you are, I will make you worse, however, if I treat you as though what you are capable of becoming I will help you become that"

– Johann Goethe, German Playwright and Author

Everyone in their life needs somebody to expect greatness from them. It is absolutely essential, and when a person knows that someone expects greatness from them it is such a powerful feeling. It eliminates doubts, fears, and concerns of that person because they know that someone believes in them and someone thinks that they can succeed.

As leaders of teams, whether we are a captain of an athletic team or a group in school or running a business or running a financial advising practice or running our family we have to realize that we can't accept people for their current state because we are always evolving, we are always progressing, we are always improving and we should be striving to get to that next level. It is our objective to not accept them for who they are but rather treat them as though they are capable of becoming what we know they can become.

And so it is the parent who doesn't treat the 10 year old like a 10 year old but rather says, "I'm going to treat you like a 12 year old and the reason that I am treating you a little above your age is so you develop and start becoming more mature." It is the giving out of responsibility. It's the coach who doesn't treat that brand new person as a freshman or a rookie but tries to make him grow. It's going to be day one right away I have a choice today. I can treat you like a rookie or I can treat you like a veteran. I hold veterans to certain standards. I am not going to be as forgiving and I'm not going to expect you to make rookie mistakes and all those things.

In our particular business of running a financial advising firm on day one when new advisors come in, I tell them I have a choice, I can treat them as a day one financial advisor or I can treat them like a top producer in this firm. I can start creating the expectation that you will make a mark on this business from today forward, because if I do, that I will help you become a top advisor. I ask them what they would prefer that I do, and almost everyone says to treat them in terms of what I am capable of becoming and we agree upon that.

So now when they are setting their goals and objectives and they are always lofty, it's fine. As a coach and their leader, it is my obligation to them to be a good coach. If I can get them to hit those goals and objectives, it's a permission slip that allows them to hit their goals. I can be tougher, if you will, as long as it comes from a foundation of love and support. You have to prove that you are being tough because you want them to succeed. So that's the main lesson: If we accept people for who they are, we will make them worse but if you treat them in terms of helping them become what they are capable of becoming they will ultimately become that.

I tell people that it is my responsibility to work with someone to help them reach their goals and objectives. With each person I work with, the very first thing I do is share Johann Goethe's quote with them and then I explain what my objective is and why I'm doing it. We selected each other. That coach selected that player, that employer selected that employee and visa-versa. They selected each other because they believe that together they could do some pretty spectacular things together. A leader has to have high expectations, which must come from a foundation of love.

CHAPTER 32:
Think of E.T.
A Leader Gets What They Exemplify and Tolerate

When I say "E.T." people automatically think of the movie **E.T.** by Steven Spielberg. What I mean is that a leader gets what they (E) exemplify and (T) tolerate. It ties into the law of limited performance. People soon discover the level of performance you will settle for as their leader and then they gravitate to that level and that's the toleration point.

Now as the leader what do you tolerate? As you have high expectations for others and are not going to tolerate anything below that expectation, you will help that person reach their goals.

I remember when I was in college, I'm embarrassed to say, but my first week of class my objective was to figure out what the toleration level was of that professor, what their expectation was of the student (what you could get away with). We've all been there whether it be a coach, teacher, parent, boss, an employer and business partner, you name it, we are always in this gauging of what is maybe the least amount of input we can put in to get the maximum output. The path of least resistance, which is the way we are hardwired.

So I am embarrassed to say that I would go into class and let's face it, some teachers were more demanding than others, some coaches, some employers, you name it, fill in the blank, some captains, some teammates, whatever that level of expectation was you somehow figure it out and you rose to it. As I mentioned earlier there were times that I would get A's in classes but they weren't very challenging but then there were times when I got C's in classes where the professors were demanding and I worked very hard and I actually felt like I had accomplished something. I had to fight tooth and nail for that C+ but the A was almost given to me and leaders have to recognize that.

What is a leader's toleration level? For example, if we are not getting the results we want at times it's a mirror test, let's look in the mirror and see what is the level of expectation that we established? We might be the problem. The reason we are not winning, the reason we are not hitting those goals, the reason we are not hitting our quarterly projections, the reason we are not getting that certain thing is because we haven't established a strong enough level of performance. We are tolerating behaviors, habits, attitude, effort, and the goals required to hit those things.

An example of this I have seen is by a gentleman by the name of Jaime Escalante and they made a movie about him in the late 80s, **Stand and Deliver**. Edward James Olmos played in the movie. It was a true story; Jaime was a math teacher in Garfield High School in East Los Angeles. The school was literally failing, they were thinking of taking the school's certification away because the students were scoring so low on the standardized tests. Escalante actually had the courage to build a mathematics program where the goal was to get students at that high school prepared to take the advanced placement calculus test.

Now, less than 1% of all students nationally get college credit because they pass the advanced placement calculus test, so this is pretty tough stuff here. And this was at the poorest, most challenged school districts in the country but this guy had a mission. He said; I believe because the students will gravitate to the level of expectation that I lay out. So he told the students that this is the journey they were on and they paid the price, made the sacrifices, they went before school, they went after school, they spent summers taking math classes and in 1982 they had 18 students pass the advanced placement calculus test. It was more than any other school in the state of California and because of that it was assumed they had cheated. "There is no way that kids from this school are passing this test better than the private schools, it can't happen." So they actually made the students retake the test and they all passed again.

The story continues, in 1987, 87 students in that school passed the advanced placement calculus. What a beautiful example of setting expectations and it truly is building a high performance, no excuse culture.

That's what leaders do; think of ET, they get what they exemplify. What do leaders exemplify in their own lives? Do they have the right attitude? Do they put forward the right amount of effort? Do they lead by example in their actions, thoughts and words? And when leaders set expectations, draw lines and don't tolerate things below those lines they create a high performance, no excuse culture where they can literally change people, change environments, and change results for the better.

One of my personal heroes is a gentlemen whose name is Maury Stewart and he is a legend in the insurance based financial services industry. Maury has truly lived a life of significance. My life is better because of Maury, much better, for that matter because Maury did something very special over 50 years ago. He hired and mentored my mentor Phil Richards. Without doing that I would not have been mentored by Phil and I cannot imagine my life without either of these 2 gentlemen. Maury said something years ago that has always stayed with me and I think of it often. Maury shared that "always remember that you might be the only bible someone reads today."

Maury is a spiritual person, however regardless of one's level of spirituality or religious beliefs or views, one can understand the nature of this incredibly powerful message. The message is simple – YOU are the example for others. That is what leadership is about. Whatever you exemplify, whatever you tolerate will become your legacy.

Maury is a perfect example of a leader exemplifying the life someone can lead. The people Maury has mentored and the impact they've had on the world has cast a ripple on so many lives it is simply remarkable. Many people in this world are better off because of Maury and they will never know his name.

ED, MAURY STEWART AND PHIL RICHARDS

PART 6:

Quick Hits

CHAPTER 33:

Provide More Service Than You Get Paid For

Whatever job, assignment, or task you are charged with; always try to deliver more than what is expected of you. When you do, you end up impressing your boss and you stand out as someone who delivers and achieves good results. You become irreplaceable because everyone wants that type of person on their team. In a world where it seems so easy to be a number and not stand out, going above and beyond expectations is a sure way to get noticed. Regardless of the size of the project, if you do it with pride and effort, it becomes noble.

CHAPTER 34:

Don't Reinvent - Implement

Don't reinvent, implement. There are many systems that have proven they work and whether it is a fitness program, a diet/nutrition plan, a system to learn a second language or to pass a test or certification. Systems are created, that if followed, will get the results one is looking for. The challenge is that we all feel the need to individualize and customize, which leads to modification of these systems and in essence reinventing something that does not have a track record of any kind and is different from the system that yielded the successful results.

The key is not to reinvent but rather just focus ones energy on implementation. The next time you see something that is getting the results that you want, have the discipline to follow the system and focus on the implementation as it was intended. You will be pleasantly surprised with the results.

CHAPTER 35:

Favorite vs. Underdog

We live in a society that roots for the underdog. We like the Hollywood stories of Rocky, Rudy, and Cinderella. But let's go back to the terms - the favorite is the one that is expected to win and the underdog is the one that is expected to lose. I do love a good Hollywood story, but when it comes to real life, I want to be the favorite.

Whatever situation you are in, you should always want to be the favorite. When you are the favorite, it means that you have done many things right, so the odds are in your favor. People look at you and predict that you will be victorious. It might not be a blockbuster storyline when the favorite wins, but let's face it - the favorite wins a lot more often than the favorite loses. You should always stack the odds in your favor. Be the favorite in all that you do.

CHAPTER 36:

Simple to Understand - Hard to Do

Many people falsely believe that something that is simple to understand is easy to do. Being physically fit involves a combination of exercising daily and eating healthy. That is simple to understand. Following through with it, on the other hand, demands lots of time and energy.

Another example is having a successful relationship with someone. Again, that is simple to understand. Put their needs before your own, be an active listener, support them, be there in times of need, but again, it's not so easy to do.

Often, the simpler something is to understand, the harder it is to do because it requires a mastery of the fundamentals, which requires discipline and persistency. The key to success is forming the habits that will help you execute these difficult tasks.

CHAPTER 37:

Would You Invest in You?

We often find ourselves in the position of asking someone for a favor - an opportunity or an exception to be made for us. When doing this, we need to stop and look at ourselves in the mirror. Would you invest in you?

If you were the person who had to make the decision to grant yourself a favor by making an exception, would you give it to yourself? Think about what the person you're asking a favor of knows about you and has seen you do in your work. If you were that person who had made those observations, would you make an exception for yourself? If your answer is yes - you would invest in you - then it is the right moment to ask for a favor.

CHAPTER 38:
Pleasure VS Happiness - What Are You Seeking?

Often, we confuse pleasure for happiness, but pleasure is a momentary state. Pleasure is taking a bite of your favorite food or watching your favorite sports team beat their arch rival. Pleasurable moments are enjoyable, but they pass quickly, and once they pass you are left to face reality. Consequently, happiness does not have to be a momentary state but instead can be a permanent mindset.

Earlier in the book, we concluded that everyone has complete control over their attitude. Happiness is indeed an attitude issue. Regardless of the momentary situation, you can always adopt an attitude of happiness. It may not always be easy to do depending on your situation and outside factors, but it is a choice you have.

Strive for a permanent state of happiness in your daily attitude. Knowing the difference between a moment of pleasure and making a decision in the present will allow you to be in a state of happiness permanently.

CHAPTER 39:

What is Invaluable is Invisible

Valuables are visible. What we often believe are valuable things in life are visible and tangible - cars, homes, jewelry, clothes, etc. These things can be seen and touched. Invaluable things are invisible. It is the love we receive from and give to others. It is the time we spend with our loved ones, it is the air we breathe, it's good health, it is the ability to think and care and create. All of these things are invisible but absolutely invaluable.

Focus on the invisible things in your life and take inventory of them. If you want to prosper there is only one way to do it - count your blessings.

CHAPTER 40:

Water Always Defeats the Rock

One of the greatest lessons that nature provides for us is the lesson of persistence and patience. We see the miracle of nature in the beauty of the Grand Canyon. That amazing world of wonder was created over millions of years of constant pressure from the flowing water against the rock. The water carved out canyons and spectacular rock formations. The rough, rigid, unbreakable rock was washed away, worn down and smoothed out over time from the constant flowing of the water.

We need to remember this when dealing with difficult situations. The lesson is that we need to keep pressure on and be patient. Water always defeats the rock. Stay persistent, patient and flowing.

CHAPTER 41:

One Demonstrates Gratefulness by Being Responsible

It isn't hard to know if someone truly appreciates something in their life. The easiest way is to see if they are responsible is with whatever it is they profess to be grateful for. It is the grandchild that works extra hard getting excellent grades because she is grateful for the gift of education that she received from her grandparents, who paid for her college tuition. It is the student-athlete that puts in extra time to practice and watch film to be a better player and teammate as he is grateful for the athletic scholarship he received. It is the employee that takes extra care in the work she does for her employer because she is grateful for the opportunity of employment.

When one is truly grateful for whatever it is in their life, they demonstrate it by being responsible with what is it they are grateful for. Are you demonstrating your gratefulness by being as responsible as you can for what it is you are grateful for? Actions speak louder than words.

CHAPTER 42:

Behave Your Way to the Top

A dear friend once said to me, "You have to act it to be it!" If you want to be an enthusiastic person, you have to act enthusiastic. If you want to be a loving and caring individual, you have to act loving and caring. If you want to be successful, you have to act successful. Acting is all about behaviors.

If you want to get to the top of your game, you have to act or behave in the manner that will get you there. Do you want to be a great student? Then act like a great student and behave the way great students behave. Want to be a great athlete? Act like a great athlete. Develop the habits and behaviors of those at the top.

CHAPTER 43:

Good, Fast and Cheap

Years ago, I saw a sign that really intrigued me. It read "Good, Fast, Cheap - Pick Any Two." When I thought about it, I realized that what that sign was really saying was, you can't have it all. Instead, you get what you pay for. If you want a product that is good and you want to get it fast, chances are it will not be cheap and you will have to pay more money to have it delivered fast. If you want something fast and cheap, it will most likely not be high in quality. If you want something good and cheap, it will probably not get to you very fast.

No matter how you look at it, that simple sign captured the lesson that you get what you pay for, and therefore expectations have to be realistic. That's how the world works.

CHAPTER 44:

No Snowflake Feels Responsible for the Avalanche

Everyone is either part of the solution or part of the problem. A great way to remember this lesson is, no snowflake feels responsible for the avalanche. One small snowflake probably did not directly cause the avalanche, but it did play a part as the avalanche was the compounding effect of each and every snowflake. One snowflake, however, did serve as the tipping point which triggered the avalanche.

In sports, a team loss may have been the result of a particular play or a certain player's mistake, but clearly, throughout the game, a series of mistakes and bad plays occurred that added to the compounding effect of the loss.

We all need to take responsibility for our actions, decisions, and attitudes and know that they all contribute to the eventual outcomes in our lives. When things go wrong and we do not get the results we wanted, it is hard to pinpoint each snowflake that contributed. Some snowflakes stand out more than others, but we know they all played a part. The key is to recognize this and to eliminate as many of these potential snowflakes as soon as possible. We all play a part in the successes or failures of our projects, even though specific contributions are not always obvious.

CHAPTER 45:

FILO

FILO - First In, Last Out. Leadership begins with being the example that you want to see in others and demonstrating the behaviors that you expect of those you lead. You must lead with example to earn the trust and respect of those you lead. The acronym FILO serves as a reminder to lead by example. Be the first one into work and the last one to leave. The captain of the football team is the first to practice and the last to leave. The CEO is the first one to start work each day and the last one to shut down. Leadership is so much about demonstrating the right habits and behaviors for others to see as the example. By being the first one in and the last one out, you set a good pace for others to run at.

CHAPTER 46:
Problem vs. Inconveniences

All too often we confuse problems with inconveniences. Allow me to explain. Life is full of inconveniences. Cars breakdown, weather causes plane delays, we lose cell phones, we forget things, we stumble on exams, and we make mistakes in personal relationships sometimes. All of these may seem like major problems when they happen and it may seem like the world is crashing down on us, but we need to keep these inconveniences in perspective. Life is difficult, and if we remember that we will be better able to handle bad things when they occur. We will also be able to celebrate and appreciate the good things in our lives.

Problems are much larger than inconveniences. A problem is losing your health. When a parent finds out their child has cancer that is a real life problem. If a student has three exams in one day that is an inconvenience that may make her life a little more hectic for a few days, but it is not a problem.

The next time you are late for something, or are stuck in an airport for a few hours, or catch a cold, remember that these are not problems but minor inconveniences. Yes, most of us will encounter serious problems, but we all have to make sure that we know the difference between problems and inconveniences so we can keep perspective on things.

CHAPTER 47:

Evolution vs. Change

We have all heard of the adages regarding change. Change or perish. Change is the only certainty we have; we cannot expect different results unless we change. The list goes on and on. Change is both a very exciting and very threatening process. We are creatures of habit, and in a world of uncertainty, we like to have certainty. To make change more acceptable, it is best to introduce it as an evolution. Most often, the change we create is not going to be true change - a 180 degree turnaround. Rather, the change we create is usually a modification or adjustment of an evolution to improve the process of that evolution.

Evolving depicts feelings, growth, progress, and advancement. Change can sometimes depict feelings of failure, fear, concern, and uncertainty. So you must first ask yourself if it is change or evolution. Then, position it in a manner that allows you to get the results you are striving to accomplish.

CHAPTER 48:
For Every "YES" There Must be a "No"

For every "yes" there is a "no." Often, when I mention this, most people think I am referring to the law of large numbers. They assume this because sales have always been a numbers game, and the more people you ask to buy your product, the more likely you are to get good results.

A piece of advice that people give is that every "no" gets you closer to a "yes." This is great advice and I strongly believe in it. In this chapter, however, we are discussing a different situation. Every time we say yes to something, it will most likely mean saying no to something else. For example, saying yes to go bowling with your friends on Tuesday night means saying no to an evening with your family. Saying yes to hanging out with your friends for an hour means saying no to your afternoon workout. Saying yes to the high calorie desert means saying no to your commitment to eat healthier.

The point here is not that you cannot have any fun. You most certainly can have fun. The point is that you must realize that when you say yes to one thing you are saying no to something else. The lesson here is to be cognizant of this each time you make a decision. Ask yourself if what you are saying yes to aligns with your priorities and values. By asking yourself this question before making a big decision, you will be able to stay on track and get the results you are striving for in your life.

CHAPTER 49:

Good Decision Making – Just Do the Right Thing

We have heard it before from the famous Vince Lombardi speech. "Winning is not a sometime thing; it is an all-time thing. You don't win once in a while, you don't do things right once in a while, you do them right all the time. Winning is a habit." The same can be said of good decision making. Good decision making is an all-time thing. I have observed that sometimes people fall into the trap of thinking that because they've made many good decisions that it perhaps gives them permission to make a bad one and the good ones will wash over or make up for the bad ones.

Unfortunately the world does not count the frequency of the good decision making or see good decision making as a bank account. In a bank account you have deposits and withdrawals. Many small deposits do not make up for 1 big withdrawal. A person may have a perfect driving record and be arrested for driving under the influence. The good decision making may play a small part of lessening the fine, but in no way will the courts say they will get off scott free because they had a perfect driving record.

Every decision must and will stand on its own. Good decision making becomes a habit. Like we have learned and discussed throughout this entire book that the most successful individuals in the world are in the HABIT FORMATION business. The more a person can make good decisions in all areas of their life, from big decisions to the very smallest, the more they have trained themselves and formed the habit of good decision making.

Again, the discipline needs to shine through with good decision making. A way to stay focused on making good decisions in every aspect of your life is to constantly be reminded yourself of just doing the next right thing. Perhaps you just had an argument with a dear friend or loved one. The next right thing would be to apologize. It would be to set aside differences and pride and simply apologize. For the student that just received a C- on an exam, the next right thing would be to visit with the teacher and review the aspects of the exam so they can improve and score better on the next exam. For the sales executive that didn't get the account, the next right thing would be to pick up the phone and begin prospecting for another account instead of feeling sorry for himself.

If one can obtain the discipline and focus to begin building up momentum by simply doing the next right thing, they will quickly get back on track on their journey to success.

FINAL CHAPTER:

Get Rich Quick: Count Your Blessings

We have a tendency to often focus on the few things we don't have in our lives at the expense or mistake of overlooking or neglecting ALL of the wonderful blessings we do have and enjoy on almost a constant basis. We forget that most of the precious gifts we have in life have been freely given to us. We have our health, our ability to think, to love, to walk, run, laugh, cry, forgive, breathe, see, hear, touch, taste, the list goes on and on and on. We overlook the loving relationships we have, the fact that we have opportunities, a school we attend, a team we play on, or a company we work for or lead.

An exercise I learned a long time ago is to take a few moments in a quiet place with a pad of paper and a pen and to begin to write all the gifts, blessings, things we are thankful and grateful for in our lives. It doesn't take long for one to see that that list far outweighs the few items a person does not have or the few inconveniences they are experiencing at the moment. This exercise brings perspective and quickly has the impact it is intended to have - to allow one to understand they are indeed RICH. There really is only one true way to get quick rich and that is to take inventory of all the good that is going on in one's life and to count their blessings.

Years ago I came across a "quiz" that I have found extremely helpful in maintaining the right perspective, having an attitude of gratitude and keeping with the "spirit" of counting my blessings:

1. Name the 5 wealthiest people in the world.
2. Name 10 people who have won the Nobel or Pulitzer Prize.
3. Name the last 5 winners of the Miss America contest.
4. Name the last 5 Heisman trophy winners.
5. Name the last half dozen Academy Award winners for best actor.
6. Name the last decade's worth of World Series winners.

How did you do?

The point is that none of us remember the headliners of yesterday. These are no second-rate achievers. They are the best in their fields. This is what our society puts on a pedestal. These are the rich, the smart, the beautiful and the athletic. But the applause dies. Awards tarnish. Achievements are forgotten. Accolades and certificates are buried with their owners.

Here is another quiz. See if you fare better with this one.

1. List a few teachers who aided your journey through school.
2. Name 3 friends who have helped you through a difficult time.
3. Name 5 people who have taught you something worthwhile.
4. Think of a few people who have made you feel appreciated and special.
5. Think of 5 people you enjoy spending time with.
6. Name half a dozen heroes whose stories have inspired you

Chances are you did much better this time and the reason is:

The people who make a difference in your life are not the ones with the most credentials, the most money, or the most awards.

They are the ones who care.

I would encourage you to take a few moments now and think of the wonderful relationships that you have in your life. For that matter write out the following statement on a piece of paper:

I cannot imagine my life without...........

Take a few minutes and let your mind wonder. Begin writing down the names of everyone that you feel has had an impact to some degree in your life. Begin writing down the organizations, institutions, places, events that also complete that sentence above.

These my friends are the blessings, these are the people, places, moments and experiences that enrich our lives. Cherish these and nurture these as they will constantly bring you a sense of peacefulness and joy.

CLOSING COMMITMENT:

YOUR BIG TROPHY DAY

I hope you remember Big Trophy Day, the story about my son Jake who set a goal to win a "big trophy" and was successful in reaching his goal. That story serves as a great example as what we can achieve when we have a goal that means something to us. We all have a "big trophy day" in us. Deep down we have something special we want to accomplish, do, experience, and be remembered for. What we need to do is to identify what that "big trophy day" is and how we are going to get there.

At North Star, the firm I have the honor and privilege of leading, we have a tradition we do each year at the New Year. Our advisors are given 2 standard envelopes and 2 pieces of paper. They are asked to write down the two most important goals they would like to accomplish in the upcoming year. 1 of the goals should be business/professional related. The other needs to be a personal goal. It is encouraged that the goals be what they would consider that if accomplished they would consider the year a success. They are to write the goals on both pieces of paper and then place the goals written on the paper in each one of the envelopes. On the envelope they are to write the date it needs to be opened. In most cases it is January 1st the following year but it could be any date that aligns with the goal.

The first envelope is for them. We tell them to place that envelope somewhere they can see it every single day. In my case the envelope sits on the corner of the bookcase that is right near my desk in my Minneapolis office. Every time I walk to my desk I see the envelope and I stop for a moment and think of the two goals and then focus on what I have done and will continue to do that day to make progress to the 2 most important goals I have for the year that if accomplished the year will be considered a success. You may recall from an earlier chapter that there is no such thing as time management but rather priority management. By doing this exercise and being able to see the envelope every day with your goals in it, it helps reinforce that we need to prioritize and make sure we are dedicating the time and energy required to hit our goal.

On the second envelope which is an exact copy of the first again we ask that one write down the date the envelope should be opened. In addition we also ask that to write down the NAME of the person they are going to give the envelope to. Then they state the following: "I have written down 2 very important goals that I am completely focused on in this upcoming year. I put them in this envelope with the name of the person that I would like to have open the envelope on the date listed. Would you do me the honor and open this envelope up on the day indicated and reach out to me to see how I did towards reaching my goal. Knowing you will be opening this envelope will help hold me accountable and keep me even more focused on reaching these important milestones because of the respect, trust, love and admiration, I have for you."

It takes courage to do an exercise like this. To inform others of our goals, dreams, and aspirations is a fearful event sometimes because we do not want to look like a failure if we do not reach what we set out to do. However, I hope from reading these pages over the past few hours you will begin to see the only failure is in not fully trying and in not having your very own big trophy day. As we shared, often times there is victory in defeat. I personally have done this exercise each year for the past decade and have only reached both of my goals on three occasions. I am batting .300 if you will. But the other seven times I missed I noticed that having the goals and striving to hit them every day and making progress put me on the doorstep of hitting them. I know with confidence that if I had not done this exercise that I would have been nowhere near hitting them. It is not the end of the world if you shoot for the stars and end up hitting the moon. It still ends up being a pretty good year and more importantly the journey was fun, challenging and many lessons were learned.

In addition to having those within our firm do this exercise I have encouraged thousands of others to do the same when I am asked to speak. I am always surprised and delighted when I receive emails from those that follow through on the envelope exercise and email to inform me that the exercise served them well. I have included two of them that I believe capture the range of the impact this activity has. I have taken the liberty to remove their identity but I wanted to give you a brief background on both. One is an extremely successful financial services leader who frankly runs one of the largest and most respected firms in the industry. His leadership and influence is known throughout the entire industry. Here is his email:

> *Ed*
> *On March 17th, 2008 (at our Board Meeting last year), You asked everyone to write down an important goal, to seal it in an envelope, and have someone that we designate other than ourselves open it after January 1st of 2009. You asked each of us to keep it on our desk in order to remind us that we had something important to accomplish that year. After coming off a very difficult year (2007) which included the departure of two managers with eight good producers, the outlook for 2008 was bleak. My future depended on our ability as a firm to turn things around by recruiting new Management and Associates.*
> *Alan Press opened the envelope on Monday January 5th (The day after I returned from vacation). My SMART Goal was as follows: "By December 31st 2008, I will have recruited 16 new Associates to build my agency." I am happy to report that we did just that, we added 16 new associates of which two are in management, grew the organization by a net 20%, and increased our life production by 8% over 2007. We are stronger now than we were before that group left. Thank you for helping me stay focused on*

> *the basics, the most important thing we need to do each day. Thank you.*

The next email was from a college student-athlete that took the envelope exercise to heart and sent me the following:

> *Mr. Deutschlander -*
> *I am writing to thank you for encouraging me to write down a pair of goals for the second half of 2009. You spoke at a student-athlete banquet for Gustavus Adolphus College down in Saint Peter around May and encouraged all of us to do so. I wrote down a pair of goals and sealed them up in the envelope you provided and didn't open the envelope until today (Jan 1) and sure enough, I achieved both goals (passing 2 of the 4 CPA exam tests and having $10K in my checking account).*
> *I just wanted to let you know that I am thankful for your advice and intend to continue goal-setting in the future.*
> *Best of luck in 2010.*

The point to sharing these two brief emails is that it works! Whether one is leading a multi-million dollar enterprise with years of worldly experience and wisdom or a college student looking at shaping and molding their present and future—it works!

So this is where it comes to you taking action and making that first step in becoming the very best version of yourself. It begins with you being the first believer in that you can live the life you have imagined for yourself. The rest of our days are indeed unwritten and you are the author of that blank page every morning when you arise. Take the first step towards the giant you have awakened within and challenge yourself with the envelope exercise. Bring to life your big trophy day and use the lessons from this book that were learned and reinforced. Remember we all need someone to expect greatness from us. Others truly believe in you, now you must believe in yourself… **Be the First Believer!**

ABOUT THE AUTHORS

Ed Deutschlander

Ed Deutschlander is currently the CEO Elect at North Star Resource Group which is one of the nation's largest and oldest privately-held independent financial advising firms. North Star has over $4 Billion of client assets entrusted to them and their origins trace back to 1908 in the Twin Cities community.

In 2002 Ed became the youngest Managing Partner nationally for the Minnesota Life's Securian Advisor Network which has over 50 advising firms throughout the country.

Ed is the Past President of GAMA International (2007-2008). GAMA International serves the professional development needs of individuals and companies engaged in the ethical distribution of financial services and products. GAMA provides its members access to networking opportunities with industry leaders, quality professional development products, and prestigious recognition awards. Members are skilled field and home office distribution leaders who are responsible for more than 90,000 advisors/agents who serve 41 million clients. Ed was asked to serve on the Board of Directors in 2001 at the age of 29 and became the youngest board member in the 50 year history of GAMA International. Ed has also been published in numerous publications whose topics include recruiting, leadership selection, training and development of financial advisors. In addition Ed is frequently and heavily quoted throughout the financial services industry. His "Recruiter's Creed" is often used and cited at industry meetings and events.

Ed is recognized as one of the premier recruiters in the financial services industry. Ed is the creator of "Recruiting University" and "Do Well by Doing Good". These two products have educated and been used by thousands of financial services leaders. Since 1998 at the age of 27, Ed has been hired as a consultant by many of the largest insurance companies in the world to help them better their recruitment, training and leadership development programs. Ed has been asked to present internationally in China, Thailand, Singapore, South America, and Canada and has literally educated tens of thousands of managers and advisors in the financial services industry giving over several hundred professional presentations. North Star's training program is featured in two New York Times Best Sellers, What the Dog Saw by Malcolm Gladwell and Use Your Head To Get Your Foot In The Door by Harvey Mackay.

Ed was the first recipient of the North Star Resource Group's Medal of Honor which recognizes servant leadership, selflessness, service and integrity. Ed was recognized as Minnesota Life Insurance Company's Recruiter of the Year every year he was eligible and since that time under his guidance and tutelage he has trained two recipients of that prestigious award. Ed has been a keynote speaker at LIMRA's (Life Insurance Marketing and Research Association) and GAMA's annual meeting and has addressed groups at MDRT (Million Dollar Round Table) and NAIFA's (National Association of Insurance and Financial Advisors) annual meetings. Ed has won numerous management awards from GAMA International and in 2002 was the only person in the industry of the 5,000 members eligible to receive the Career Development Award Platinum level. Ed holds the CLU (Chartered Life Underwriter) and CLF (Chartered Leadership Fellow) designations and was at the time the youngest person to achieve the CLF designation awarded by the American College. In 2008 Ed was recognized by NAIFA as one of the "4 under 40" award winners for his career accomplishments and in 2010 was named by The Minneapolis/ St. Paul Business Journal's as one of the "40 under 40" award winners.

COMMUNITY INVOLVEMENT

In 2004 Ed was asked to serve as one of the founding board members of the Scott Richards North Star Charitable Foundation (SRNSCF). The SRNSCF donates annually to the following charities; Breast Cancer, Ataxia, Cystic Fibrosis, Alzheimer's, Myleofibrosis. Ed and his wife, Toni, founded and championed the Twin Cities Bikes for Kids program in 2004. Bikes for Kids makes it possible for disadvantaged youth to receive a brand new bike complete with a helmet and lock at a surprise holiday party hosted annually at the Twin Cities Metrodome. In the past nine years, over 3,200 children in the Big Brothers/Big Sisters greater Twin Cities program have received this holiday gift and surprise.

PERSONAL

Ed is a 1993 graduate of Macalester College in St. Paul Minnesota where he played, started and lettered in two varsity sports (Football and Baseball) and served as Captain of his college football team. In addition to his professional and industry commitments Ed enjoys speaking to and educating today's college students. Ed is asked to speak at universities and colleges around the country on life after college and sharing lessons on leadership and personal development to assist them in their life endeavors after college.

Ed resides in Carver Minnesota with his wife of 22 years, Toni, and their four children Ashley, Jacob, Hannah and William.

For more information:

Ed Deutschlander
CEO Elect at North Star Resource Group
Ed@northstarfinancial.com
www.northstarfinancial.com

ABOUT THE AUTHORS

Rich Campe

Rich Campe, CEO, Founding Partner and Master ProAdvisor Coach, is an avid entrepreneur, with 21 years of international and domestic Sales and Sales Management experience, bestselling author and a graduate from North Central College in Naperville, IL with a double major in marketing and communications.

Rich founded Rich Campe International, Corporate and Personal Coaching, which is now Rich Campe International/ DBA ProAdvisorCoach. Rich is a serious entrepreneur who has started, owned and sold Verizon Cellular stores, Real-estate companies and nutritional companies, to name a few. Rich has served as a board member for SMU (Southern Methodist University) MBA mentor program and has been invited to speak at multiple business conferences where he has shared the stage with world and business leaders such as President George Bush Sr., Les Brown, Tony Robbins, Zig Ziglar and a host of other CEO's and influential leaders.

Rich graduated as a Certified Coach with Tony Robbins in 1991 and served as part of the original Jim Rohn International Coaching team for several years. Rich is a very successful business owner and entrepreneur; however, his real passion lies in helping people reach their true potential. ProAdvisorCoach clients include a host of companies such as... Bank of America, Woodbury Financial, Northwestern Mutual, AXA, Ameriprise, Hartford Financial, Planco and ING to name a few.

Rich has a clear passion for business entrepreneurialism that brings good fortune to all that he is involved with, and his passions don't stop at business. Rich is a Certified First Degree Black Belt in Martial Arts. When he isn't chasing down opportunity, he can be found hanging with the family, who give dad a run for his money... biking, snowboarding, wakeboarding, golfing, hiking and running with their dog Chloe!

For more information:

Rich Campe
CEO - ProAdvisorCoach
rich@ProAdvisorCoach.com
www.ProAdvisorCoach.com